ROBERT E. LEE: AN ALBUM

ROBERT E. LEE
An Album

Emory M. Thomas

W.W. Norton & Company
New York | London

The text and display of this book is composed in Janson Text;

     display numerals are set in Bodoni; credits, and running footers

     are set in FF Thesis,™ TheMix™

Interior layout and composition by John Bernstein, Brooklyn, NY

Jacket design by Lauren Graessle

Manufacturing by Friesens, Canada

Cover and frontispiece: Painting of Lee by Theodore Pine, 1904.

     Courtesy of Washington and Lee University

Library of Congress Cataloging-in-Publication Data

Thomas, Emory M., 1939 –

     Robert E. Lee : an album / Emory M. Thomas.

         p.   cm.

     ISBN 0-393-04778-4

1. Lee, Robert E. (Robert Edward), 1807 – 1870 Pictorial works.

2. Generals — Confederate States of America Biography Pictorial works.

3. Confederate States of America. Army Biography Pictorial works.

4. Lee, Robert E. (Robert Edward), 1807 – 1870 Miscellanea.

5. Generals — Confederate States of America Biography Miscellanea.

6. Confederate States of America. Army Biography Miscellanea.

I. Title.

E467.1.L4T47   1999

973.7'3'092 — dc21

[B]

W. W. Norton & Company, Inc.

500 Fifth Avenue, New York NY 10110

www.wwnorton.com

W. W. Norton & Company Ltd.

10 Coptic Street, London WC1A 1PU

1 2 3 4 5 6 7 8 9 0

Contents

He was not mild with life or drugged with justice,
He gripped life like a wrestler with a bull,
Impetuously. It did not come to him
While he stood waiting in a famous cloud,
He went to it and took it by both horns
And threw it down.

— STEPHEN VINCENT BENET, *John Brown's Body*

Acknowledgments

Here is a list of some of the gracious and capable people who have given aid and comfort to the hunting and gathering associated with producing this album. Without them, this book would not exist.

- ❖ Ann Marie Price and Bryan Clark Green at the Virginia Historical Society

- ❖ Terri Hudgins and John Coski at the Museum of the Confederacy

- ❖ Elizabeth M. Gushee and Lee Viverette at the Library of Virginia

- ❖ Lisa McCowen and C. Vaughn Stanley at the Leyburn Library, Washington and Lee University

- ❖ Julie Kline in the Development Office at Washington and Lee University

- ❖ Mandy Johnson at the Georgia Historical Society

- ❖ Mike Francis at St. Paul's Church, Richmond, Virginia

- ❖ Judy Hynson at Stratford Hall

- ❖ Lisette Voyatzis at the Tudor Place Foundation, Washington, D.C.

- ❖ Ellen Thomasson at the Missouri Historical Society

- ❖ Mary Malen and Frank Cucoruco at Arlington House

- ❖ Calder Loth at St. Paul's Church, Richmond, Virginia, and the Virginia Department of Historic Resources

- ❖ Robert K. Krick

- ❖ Junius Rhodes Fishburne

- ❖ Anne Carter Zimmer, author of *The Robert E. Lee Family Cooking and Housekeeping Book*

- ❖ and as ever, the lovely and talented Frances Taliaferro Thomas

Introduction

In several ways, this book is an extension of *Robert E. Lee: A Biography*. In the course of reading the Lee corpus in many manuscript repositories and visiting the places where Lee lived and worked and fought, I became impressed with the beauty of the places associated with this man.

Conducting research about most people and topics can be pretty dreary business. Sitting in sterile space, hunched over crumbling paper, poring over pages in darkness broken only by fluorescent tubes, working while someone bored watches to ensure the security of these sacred texts, the scholar can usually claim no aesthetic attraction for the process of research.

But Lee was different. The largest single collection of his personal papers is in the Virginia Historical Society, and the Society building is an elegant space set next to the Virginia Museum of Fine Arts, very close to Monument Avenue in Richmond, Virginia. The repositories of other collections of Lee materials are equally attractive, or even more so. I refer to Stratford Hall, Lee's birthplace and lovely, lively estate on the Northern Neck…and to Washington and Lee University in Lexington, Virginia, where Lee worked his educational wonders during the final five years of his life… and to the United States Military Academy at West Point,

1 Michael Miley made this striking photograph of Lee in Lexington in January 1870. It was one of the last, if not the last, photographs ever taken of Lee.

from which Lee graduated and to which he returned as superintendent just about twenty years later…and to the Georgia Historical Society in Savannah, locale of some of Lee's papers relating to his duties and friendships in that place…and to the Library of Virginia, which occupies new quarters and now possesses parking space…and to the Museum of the Confederacy, next to the White House of the Confederacy in downtown Richmond. The list goes on… to St. Louis, San Antonio, Washington, Arlington, Alexandria, and more sites well worth seeing. Even Lee's battlefields are now beautiful, because they are often the only sustained green space anywhere around.

I think my first (and only) wife was the first to propose a book about the pretty places associated with Lee. She had in mind a collection of attractive images linked by some direct connection with Lee. I liked that idea and expanded it to include pictures of people whom Lee knew or who knew Lee. Then I added "things" associated with Lee. Then I thought of quotations, "sound bites" by or about Lee. And then I had to include photographs and portraits of Lee himself—not all of them, since this is not an encyclopedic or remotely definitive work on the Lee image. I wanted to exhibit pictures that Lee's friends and family, and Lee himself, considered interesting or faithful likenesses. Jim Mairs, an extremely talented editor at W.W. Norton, suggested including a sample of the uses to which people have put Lee's image during the period since his death—the image of Lee's image in American life. This genre includes some very fine art and some pretty trashy kitsch, and I have included here only the smallest sample of that, which appeals to my admittedly perverse taste and earthy appreciation of tastelessness. Junius R. Fishburne, director of Stratford Hall—Lee's birthplace and once the "seat" of the Lee family—suggested including visual materials that reflect the world or at least a portion of the world that Lee saw, pictures of places and objects that would have been familiar to Lee.

This book is an album in the literal sense. It contains pictures, contemporary with Lee and with us, of places associated with Lee. It includes pictures of people Lee knew and pictures of Lee. Here is some of the visual record of what history and hucksters have done with Lee. And the album also includes images of "things," from suits to sword, that belonged to Lee, as well as words of and about him.

It is said that "every picture tells a story." Some of the images reproduced here are all but obligatory; a Lee album must include a picture of Traveller, of course. Other images are here because they trigger stories about Lee; the pictures suggest some experience in Lee's life. Thus the photographs of Cary Robinson, Henry J. Hunt, and Montgomery C. Meigs, and the prose of Beverly R. Codwise, for example, appear on these pages.

Of course, many more pictures exist that relate to the life of Lee. Paring down to the images presented here was a difficult task. These are but samples of a rich body of materials. My goal has been to offer images that are interesting, pretty, and meaningful. I know the stories are good. I hope the pictures enhance the stories and speak eloquently for themselves. ❖

Robert E. Lee
An Album

Young Man Lee

1

Robert Edward Lee was born into a long-esteemed family beset at the time with shame and genteel penury. Robert's father was head-over-heels in debt en route to debtors' prison. Henry ("Light-Horse Harry") Lee had been a hero in the American Revolution, governor of Virginia, member of Congress, and lord of the Lee "seat," Stratford Hall. But all of this fame had given place to infamy. Light-Horse Harry Lee left his family and the country when Robert was six and died when Robert was eleven.

Ann Carter Lee was a stalwart soul and a resourceful head of household. She managed to raise seven children and launch them all upon careers or marriages before she died at fifty-six, in 1829. Robert was with his mother until the end. He had just graduated from the United States Military Academy at West Point. Thereafter, he worked hard to restore the Lee family reputation. He never really knew his father, and he spent much of his life trying to know him at the same time as he was busy living down his father's rascality.

Robert Lee began his professional life as an engineer and worked at a series of construction projects for the U.S. Army. He also worked for the chief of the Engineer Corps in Washington. Lee likely never knew it, but the first step he ever took in his military career seemed some sort of evil omen. The first letter Lee ever wrote that still exists was sent to Secretary of War John C. Calhoun, accepting his appointment to West Point. Written on April 1 (April Fool's Day), 1824, the missive was rather pro forma and quite brief (two

ON PREVIOUS PAGE

< 2 | Photograph by Mathew Brady, taken April 16, 1865, at the house the Lees were renting on Franklin Street in Richmond. Courtesy of the Virginia Historical Society

3 | Cradle of Robert Edward Lee.
Courtesy of Stratford Hall

4 | Stratford Hall in a state of some disrepair, likely as it was when Robert was born in the Lee house that would pass out of the family within two decades.
Courtesy of the Museum of the Confederacy

We have very seldom more than one dish on the table, of meat, to the great discomfort of my young Ladies and Gentlemen, whom you know have various tastes—It requires a length of time every night, to determine what shall be brought next morning from market—As there is to be but one dish, all cannot be pleased: Ann [now sixteen] prefers fowls, but they are so high, that they are sparingly dealt in; and if brought to table, scarcely, a back, falls to Smith [now almost fourteen] and Robert's [now nine] share, so that they rather not be tantalized with the sight of them; and generally urge the purchase of veal; while Mildred [now five] is as solicitous, that whortleberries or cherries should compose our dinner.

— ANN CARTER LEE, May, 1816

5 | Henry ("Light-Horse Harry") Lee, father of Robert E. Lee, Revolutionary hero, governor of Virginia, member of Congress, and rascal. The elder Lee in effect deserted his family and sailed away, one step ahead of his creditors, to the West Indies. Robert spent some of his life trying to know this man who left when he was six and died when he was eleven. The portrait is by Gilbert Stuart.

Courtesy of the Library of Virginia

> **6** | Probably Ann Carter Lee, second wife of Light-Horse Harry Lee and mother of Robert Edward Lee. She is wearing a medal honoring George Washington.

Courtesy of Stratford Hall

sentences). But it certainly did not bode well for Lee in any academic setting, or for his prospects in the military. Within Lee's two sentences in the letter that essentially launched his career was a misspelled word ("honnoured").

In 1831, Robert married Mary Custis, the only child of Mary Fitzhugh Custis and George Washington Parke Custis, who was the grandson of Martha Washington and, after her marriage to George Washington, the adopted son of the first president and self-styled "child of Mount Vernon." Custis inherited considerable landed wealth from his grand-mother, and lived in style at Arlington House, just across the Potomac River from Washington. Robert had known Mary Custis from childhood, and she provided him with what he most wanted—security, status, stability, and the tradition of a loving family. Together the Lees had seven children:

George Washington Custis ("Boo"), 1832–1913
Mary Custis ("Daughter"), 1835–1918
William Henry Fitzhugh ("Rooney"), 1837–1891
Anne Carter ("Annie"), 1839–1862
Eleanor Agnes ("Wigs"), 1841–1873
Robert Edward, Jr. ("Rob"), 1843–1914
Mildred Childe ("Precious Life"), 1846–1905

7 | Ann McCarty Lee, wife of Henry Lee IV, Robert's older half-brother. These Lees inherited Stratford Hall from Henry's mother Matilda and lived there in some style during the early nineteenth century. They had a child who died tragically in a fall down the steps of the house. In her grief, Ann took to her bed and began taking narcotics to the point that she was often in an altered state of consciousness. Then something happened between Henry Lee and his sister-in-law Betsy McCarty, who was living at Stratford Hall as Lee's ward. Maybe there was a child involved; certainly there was adultery, and a subsequent scandal also impli-cated Henry Lee in the mishandling of Betsy McCarty's money. In 1822, Henry "lost the farm" in a literal sense; he had to sell Stratford Hall to appease his creditors. Henry and Ann reconciled and spent their final years in Paris. Henry, known as "Black-Horse Harry" by now, wrote one volume of a two-volume biog-raphy of Napoleon and died in 1837. Ann, still addicted to morphine, lived in poverty, supported by funds sent to her by her half-brothers-in-law, Charles Carter and Robert Edward Lee. She died tragically in 1840.

Courtesy of Stratford Hall

Bearing seven children in fourteen years took a toll upon Mary Lee. She had several periods of poor health and developed a crippling form of rheumatism that plagued her from about her mid-thirties; by her mid-fifties, Mary Lee was in a wheelchair most of the time.

Robert Lee, concerned about his wife, worked hard to find relief for her and ease her pain as much as possible. But he also compensated himself with friendships with bright young women. He flattered them, corresponded with them, and exchanged witty, sometimes risqué banter. He most probably did nothing more than this. His father's example, if nothing else, compelled Lee to maintain control of himself.

As he approached his forties in the mid-nineteenth century, Lee became more restless. Family affairs, active children, and engineering tasks occupied his time, but they no longer seemed to satisfy him. Even earlier, he had chided himself for not doing more to better himself. Actually, Lee was as successful as anyone could be in the peacetime army. He was known as the handsomest man in the army, and he was a captain at thirty-one.

When the war with Mexico began in 1846, Lee knew that he had to make his mark. He spent some frustrating time while others were winning laurels in the early battles. Then Lee got his opportunity. General Winfield Scott selected him for his staff in the campaign designed to win the war — the landing at Veracruz and the march to Mexico City. ❖

8 | Sidney Smith Lee, Robert E. Lee's older brother (born 1802), named for the family in Camden, New Jersey, that took care of Ann Lee when she went into labor en route home from Philadelphia and New York. Mary Chestnut, the famed diarist, once declared that she liked Smith better than Robert.
Courtesy of Stratford Hall

10 | Christ Church, Alexandria, Virginia. George Washington worshipped here, and on July 17, 1853, the Right Reverend John Johns confirmed Robert E. Lee, along with two of his daughters, Mary and Anne. The church, built between 1767 and 1773, and remodeled at various times since, remains an active parish.   Photograph by E. T.

9 | The Right Reverend William Meade. Elected bishop of the Diocese of Virginia, Meade usually receives credit or blame for moving the Episcopal Church into the nineteenth-century evangelical mainstream in the United States. He may have saved the Episcopal Church from extinction; after all, the successor to the Anglican Church had limited appeal in post-Revolutionary America. Then again, Evangelicalism seems to have provoked considerable mischief within the American mainstream during the nineteenth century. So Meade must reap a mixture of both praise and censure from posterity.   Courtesy of Harry T. Taliaferro III, of Warsaw, Virginia

11 | Shirley, the early home of Ann Carter Lee, Robert's mother. This estate on the north bank of the James River below Richmond is still home to the Carters, who still farm the land. Lee visited here throughout his life.

Courtesy of the Virginia Historical Society

12 | Ravensworth, Fairfax County, Virginia. This was the home of Maria and William Henry Fitzhugh, relatives of the Lees. Rooney was named for William Henry Fitzhugh, and to this place Ann Carter Lee came to die. Robert, just graduated from West Point, came to be with his mother. The Fitzhughs also owned the house at 607 Oronoco Street in Alexandria, where Robert lived for most of his boyhood.

Courtesy of the Virginia Historical Society

13 | The home and school of Benjamin Hallowell, with whom young Robert Lee studied mathematics to prepare for West Point. About his pupil Hallowell wrote, "He imparted a finish and a neatness, as he proceeded to everything he undertook. One of the branches of Mathematics he studied with me was Conic Sections, in which some of the diagrams are very complicated. He drew the diagrams on a slate; and although he well knew that the one he was drawing would have to be removed to make room for another, he drew each one with as much accuracy and finish lettering and all, as if it were to be engraved and printed." Photograph by E. T.

14 | Lee's home during most of his boyhood, 607 Oronoco Street in Alexandria, Virginia. Young Robert lived here (the house belonging to his relative William Fitzhugh) until 1825, when he left to attend West Point. Much later in his life, he climbed the fence enclosing the side yard to see if the snowball bush was still where he remembered it and whether the bush was in bloom.

Photograph by E. T.

15 | Mary Custis Lee in 1838 in her early thirties. Portrait by William E. West. Courtesy of Stratford Hall

16 | A portrait by William E. West, painted in the spring of 1838 when Lee was thirty-one years old. This was the first of three portraits of Lee done from life. Courtesy of the Virginia Historical Society

YOUNG MAN LEE

17 Harriet Randolph Hackley Talcott, wife of Lee's friend and onetime commanding officer, Andrew Talcott. Lee carried on a mock(?) affair with "my beautiful Talcott" and wrote to her soon after the birth of her first child, a girl, on behalf of his own child Custis:

"The all accomplished & elegant Master Custis Lee begs to place in her hands, his happiness & life, being assured that as for her he was born, so for her will he live. His only misery can be her frown, his only delight, her smile. He hopes that her assent will not be withheld from his most ardent wishes, & that in their blissful union Fortune may be indemnified for her miscarriage of the Affaire du Coeur of the Father & Mother." Lee knew her well enough to suggest that he was the father of her child. Courtesy of the Virginia Historical Society

18 Arlington House, the home of the Custis family and "home" to the Lees to the degree they ever had a home. George Washington Parke Custis commissioned the English architect George Hadfield to design the house. It resembles the Temple of Theseus in Athens and took fifteen years (1802–17) to build, because Custis worked in fits and starts.

Courtesy of the Virginia Historical Society

19 | George Washington Parke Custis, the grandson of Martha Washington, was adopted by George Washington. He grew up at Washington's home, Mount Vernon, and never got over the experience. He was ever after "the Child of Mount Vernon." He was Lee's father-in-law and very much different. Yet Custis had copious wealth (principally in land), his daughter adored him, and he even possessed military rank—an honorific "major." Custis dabbled in many things—poetry, drama, sheep breeding, painting, et al.—but he achieved very little. He did, however, play the role of planter-aristocrat quite well. Courtesy of Stratford Hall

YOUNG MAN LEE

21 | Robert E. Lee, Jr., third son, sixth child, born October 27, 1843. Rob remembered his father's playful nature and the tradition of tickling his feet while he read stories to the younger children.

Courtesy of the Virginia Historical Society

22 | Mildred Childe Lee, called "Precious Life," 1846–1905.
Courtesy of the Virginia Historical Society

20 | A photograph probably taken in 1845 of Lee and son Rooney. Lee was thirty-eight and Rooney eight at the time. Lee is quite the fashion plate here. His long, large sideburns, striped trousers, counter-striped vest, and hand-in-coat pose all seem a bit more pretentious than Lee usually was.

Courtesy of the Virginia Historical Society

23 This is what Savannah looked like in 1837—about six years after Lee left to take up his duties at Fort Monroe. Robert Lee left Eliza Mackay in Savannah, a young woman with whom he corresponded for most of his life. After

Lee married, Eliza Mackay wrote him the news that she was getting married herself and would soon become Eliza Mackay Stiles. Lee responded from Arlington where he and Mary Lee had gone for a visit. Soon after the date of Eliza's

wedding, Robert wrote, "How did you desport yourself, My Child? Did you go off well like a torpedo cracker on Christmas morning? …" Did Eliza Stiles know the meaning of the torpedo cracker metaphor?

Courtesy of the Georgia Historical Society

24 | Fort Pulaski near Savannah, Georgia. Lee's first assignment in the army was to prepare the foundation for this fort. He worked on the project for two years and then moved on to Fort Monroe, Virginia. Twenty-five million bricks later, the fort was ready to defend the mouth of the Savannah River.

Photograph by E.T.

26 | A view of St. Louis from the Mississippi River in 1836. Lee went to the river port in 1837 to begin some engineering projects there and upriver. He spent about four years in and around St. Louis and during one of those years brought his family west to accompany him. The Lees lived with Debby and William Beaumont and their three children in the house of William Clark (former governor and the "Clark" of the Lewis and Clark expedition to the west coast). The Clark house was then at the corner of Vine and Main Streets in what is now downtown St. Louis.

Courtesy of the Missouri Historical Society

‹ 25 | The War Department in Washington, where Lee worked when assigned to assist the Chief of Engineers. *From Battles and Leaders*

27 | Lee's drawing of the Mississippi River and St. Louis. He moved the river by building a dike from the Illinois shore to the eastern end of Bloody Island, shoring up the northeastern end of the island with a revetment and constructing a dike from the western end of the island westward. The result of these constructions was to influence the river to flow toward St. Louis and maintain the channel on the Missouri side. The scheme worked.

This drawing is in Lee's report printed in *Executive Documents*, 25th Congress, 2d Session, vol. II, no. 139

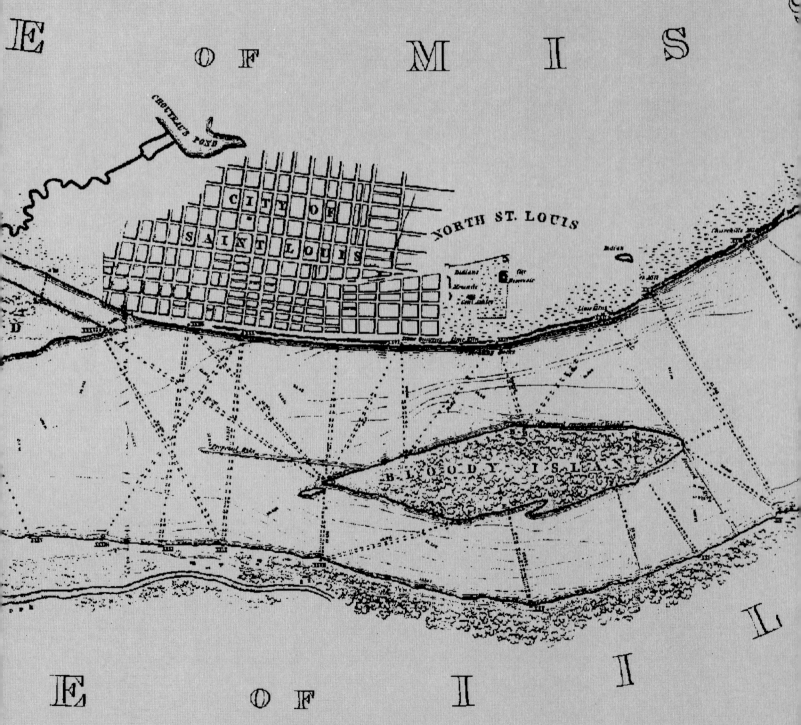

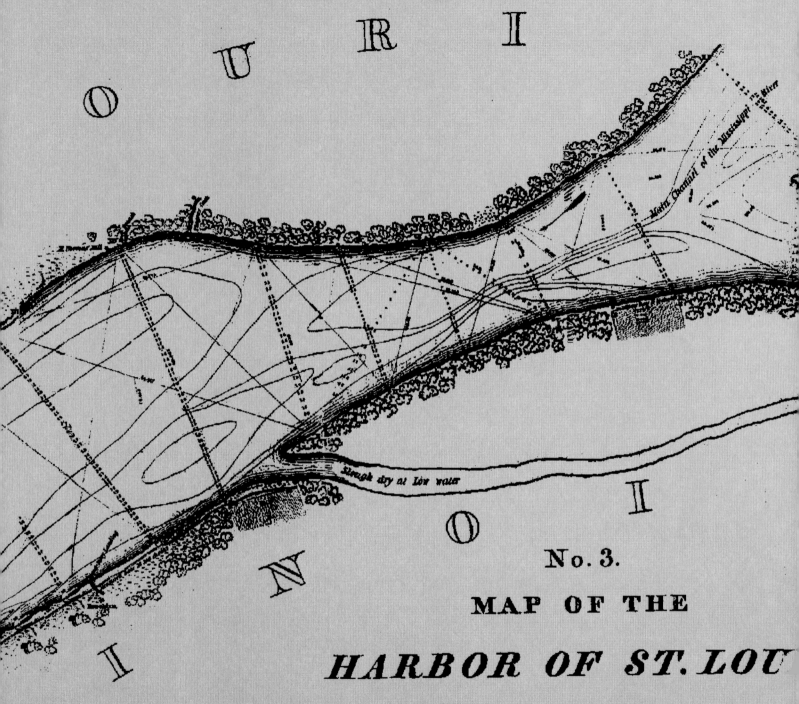

No. 3.

MAP OF THE

HARBOR OF ST. LOU

MISSISSIPPI RIVE

OCT. 1837.

Surveyed by Lt. R.E. Lee Corps of Engineers
Assisted by Lt. M.C. Meigs do.   do.
J.S. Morehead and H. Kayser
Drawn by Lt. Meigs Corps of Engineers

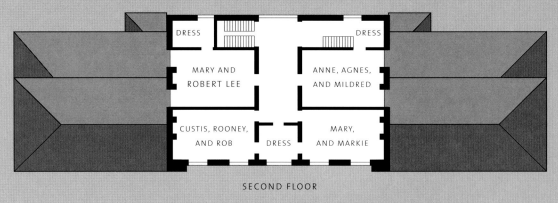

SECOND FLOOR

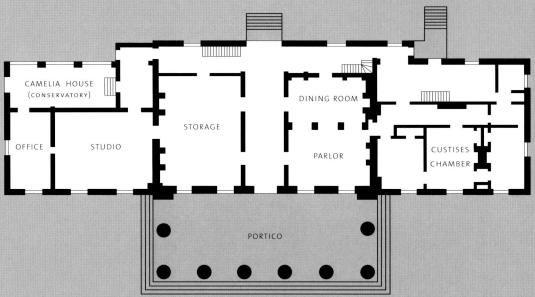

ARLINGTON HOUSE 1848–1852

Robert Lee at Midlife

2

Robert Lee first found the Mexican War in San Antonio, Texas. There he joined the army of General John Wool and eventually marched into Mexico. After about three months of considerable marching and no fighting, Lee received orders to join Winfield Scott's army; on his fortieth birthday, he set out toward Scott's headquarters and destiny.

Scott first conducted an amphibious assault on Veracruz; Lee was prominent among the officers who placed and worked the artillery during the campaign. Next Scott led his army inland and confronted the Mexican army of General Antonio Lopez de Santa Anna at Cerro Gordo. It was Lee who found a route into the rear of the Mexican defensive position, and he personally guided a division of the United States force to the point of attack. The attacks were successful, and Lee became a hero of the Battle of Cerro Gordo in 1847. The march toward Mexico City continued, and in the Battles of Contreras and Churubusco, Lee again distinguished himself, this time by finding a passage through the Pedregal, an expanse of lava that appeared impenetrable. He also contributed to the victory of United States troops at Mexico City, sustaining a wound in the process.

29 | Arlington House, the home of the Custis family and "home" to the Lees to the degree they ever had a home. George Washington Parke Custis commissioned the English architect George Hadfield to design the house. It resembles the Temple of Theseus in Athens and took fifteen years (1802–17) to build, because Custis worked in fits and starts.

Courtesy of the National Park Service

28 | Arlington House during one of the periods when the Lees lived there with the Custises. The "storage" room downstairs was devoid of furniture until the Lees installed some parlor pieces they had purchased for their quarters elsewhere. "Markie," who shared a bedroom with Mary the daughter, was Martha Custis Williams, a distant relative who was often with the family and with whom Robert Lee carried on a correspondence, both lively and tender, for almost a quarter of a century.

Drawn from material at the site as administered by the National Park Service

30 | The view from Arlington House across the Potomac River toward Washington. The Lincoln Memorial, Washington Monument, and United States Capitol are all visible in this recent photograph. Photograph by E. T.

31 | White Parlor at Arlington House, furnished by Mary and Robert Lee. The Custises used the room for storage until 1855. National Park Service

> [Children] should be governed by love not fear. When love influences the parent, the child will be activated by the same spirit.

> — ROBERT E. LEE, diary, 1857, regarding child rearing

Lee gained a distinguished record in Mexico and Scott's sincere admiration. He returned to Arlington House and immediately suffered sufficient embarrassment to keep his heroism from getting out of hand. Lee arrived in Washington by train, having been away for twenty-two months. The carriage sent to meet the conquering hero missed making a connection with Lee, so he obtained a horse from the War Department and rode across the Potomac and up the hill toward his house. As Lee approached, no one recognized the rider but the Lee family dog. Spec began barking joyfully well before anyone in the house knew who Lee was. Soon the family recognized their returning warrior and gathered at the door to greet him. Lee came into the entrance hall, hugging his children as he went, and then realized he had not acknowledged the welcome of his youngest son, Robert E. Lee, Jr. ("Rob"), who was now over four.

"Where is my little boy?" the father asked.

Lee pushed through other family members, spied a young lad, and swooped the little fellow into his arms.

> **34** A facsimile of Lee's will. He wrote this (his only will) on August 31, 1846, as he prepared to go to Mexico to participate in the war. Lee's wishes were simple. He left his estate to his wife and at her death desired his property to pass to his children, "as their Situations & necessities in life may require." Such a pregnant statement says much about Lee's estimate of his family's goodwill and concern for each member. The "Schedule of Property" reveals two facts of significance. First, Lee had considerable property in stocks and bonds. Second, Lee continued to own slaves (most likely from his mother's estate). About the middle of the page is a reference to "Nancy & her children at the White House (plantation owned by Lee's father-in-law)," whom Lee desired "liberated, so soon as it can be done to their advantage & that of others."

One copy of Lee's will is in the Virginia Historical Society

33 | Henry J. Hunt, who became a general in the Union Army but knew Lee from the time he was a lieutenant at Fort Hamilton in Brooklyn, New York. In the early 1840s, Hunt and Lee were of like mind in trying to distance themselves from a controversy within the Episcopal Church. At issue was the Oxford Movement advocating "high," more formal, more like the Roman Catholic Church, liturgical practice. The leader of this faction in the church was Edward Bouverie Pusey. At a gathering of officers at which Puseyism was a topic of discussion, Lee said to Hunt: "I am glad to see that you keep aloof from the dispute that is disturbing our little parish. That is right, and we must not get mixed up in it; we must support each other in that. But I must give you some advice about it, in order that we may understand each other. *Beware of Pussyism! Pussyism* is always bad, and may lead to unchristian feeling; therefore beware of *Pussyism!*" No one now knows for certain what Lee meant by "Pussyism." In context, the sexual slang seems to make better sense.

Brady Collection, Library of Congress

While he hugged the boy, Lee learned to his chagrin that he was Armistead Lippitt, Rob's little playmate.

His family had not recognized the returning hero until the dog had greeted Lee. And then Lee returned the recognition confusion by mistaking a neighbor for his son and namesake.

Colonel Lee lived again at Arlington House for the next few years and worked for the Chief of the Engineer Corps in Washington and elsewhere. Then he went with his family to West Point to serve as superintendent. Lee did not want the assignment and tried to avoid it; he very probably resented the stern, rote method of learning and living at the Academy. His service was relatively brief during the second period he lived on the Hudson River; Lee left in 1855 to join a cavalry regiment in Texas. He had changed his branch of army service, from engineers to cavalry, and traveled to the plains of Texas. What did Lee hope to find in this new place in this different sort of service?

Whatever Lee's expectations, what he found for the next few years was the tedium of sitting on courts-martial. For the first time in his military career, he had the opportunity to command troops. Always before, he had been on the staff of the person in command. But now that he had a command, was in effect "Marse Robert," he rarely was able to exercise authority.

Then in October 1857, Lee's father-in-law died. Lee had to abandon his command and assume the duties of executor of George Washington Parke Custis's estate. Lee left Texas—having seldom led troops and having never seen combat when he was in charge. ❖

36 | Winfield Scott, on whose staff Lee served in the Mexican War during Scott's spectacular march from Veracruz to Mexico City. Lee's reconnaissance skills and good judgment contributed significantly to Scott's victories and inspired the old general to call Lee "the very best soldier I ever saw in the field." Scott suggested that in the event of war, the United States should insure Lee's life for $5 million. In 1861, Scott, "Old Fuss and Feathers" by then, offered Lee command of the army the nation was raising to suppress the rebellion. Lee thanked his former boss and decided to cast his lot with Virginia and the Confederacy. Courtesy of the Virginia Historical Society

35 | Entrance of the army into the Grand Plaza at Mexico [City].

Edward D. Mansfield, *The Mexican War* (1848)

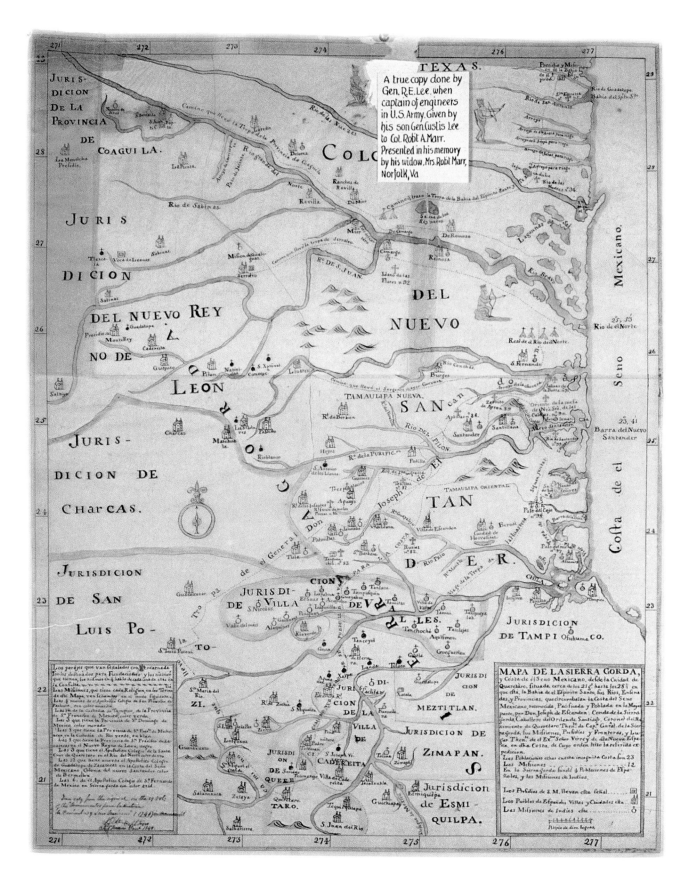

38 | Daguerreotype taken by Mathew Brady between 1850 and 1852, when Lee was between forty-three and forty-five years old. This photograph became the basis for numerous representations of Lee, including many used during the war. Courtesy of the Virginia Historical Society

39 | The Right Reverend John Johns, bishop of the Diocese of Virginia following William Meade. Reverend Johns confirmed Robert E. Lee in the Episcopal Church on July 17, 1853. At the time, Lee was forty-six years old; he had been attending church with considerable regularity since childhood, and he had already served on the vestry of a parish in Brooklyn, New York. So the obvious question is, why did Lee wait so long to join the church he was supporting and attending? The most likely answer is the simplest. Lee had never gotten around to confirmation and he did so in 1853 because two of his daughters were going to be confirmed and he thought it might be nice to join them. Courtesy of the Virginia Historical Society

General Robert E. Lee C.S.A.

37 | This is a map of a portion of Mexico copied by Robert E. Lee while he waited for the peace treaty to end the Mexican War.

Courtesy of the Museum of the Confederacy, photograph by Katherine Wetzel

ROBERT LEE AT MIDLIFE

41 | Custis Lee as a cadet at West Point. He graduated number one in his class (1854) and so surpassed his father—for the only time in his life. During his second year at the Academy (third class, sophomore), Custis complained of depression and "blues," likely a varient of the "sophomore slump" that still affects students in colleges and universities. His father responded and in so doing wrote out a credo of his own:

> Shake off those gloomy feelings. Drive them away. Fix your mind and pleasures upon what is before you.... All is bright if you will think it so. All is happy if you will make it so. Do not *dream*. It is too ideal, too imaginary. Dreaming by day, I mean. Live in the world you inhabit. Look upon things as they are. Take them as you find them. Make the best of them. Turn them to your advantage.

Robert E. Lee did follow his own counsel. He tried to make the best of all circumstances, both personally and professionally.

Courtesy of the Virginia Historical Society

There is an art in imparting…knowledge, and in making a subject agreeable to those that learn, which I have never found that I possessed, and you know the Character of Cadets well enough to be convinced that it is no easy matter to make the labor of mind & body pleasant to them.   —ROBERT E. LEE, AUGUST, 1839, about returning to West Point as an instructor

40 | The second of three portraits of Lee painted from life. This is his superintendent's portrait from his tenure at the United States Military Academy. It was painted by Robert W. Weir, who taught drawing at West Point.

Courtesy of the Virginia Historical Society

I think it however a greater evil to the white than to the black race, & while my feelings are strongly enlisted in behalf of the latter, my sympathies are more strong for the former. The blacks are immeasurably better off here than in Africa, morally, socially & physically. The painful discipline they are undergoing, is necessary for their instruction as a race, & I hope will prepare & lead them to better things. How long their subjugation may be necessary is known & ordered by a wise & merciful Providence. Their emancipation will sooner result from the mild & melting influence of Christianity, than the storms & tempests of fiery Controversy. This influence though slow is sure. The doctrines & miracles of our Saviour have required

"…Bearded like a pard, jealous in honour.…"

3

Robert E. Lee had reason to dislike his father-in-law; George Washington Parke Custis was not exactly a man obsessed with accomplishing things. He dabbled. Custis was affable, courteous, and hospitable; fortunately, he never had to be much more than that. When Lee began to think about executing the provisions of Custis's will, he discovered that his father-in-law did not write wills very well.

Custis was generous. He wished his slaves freed; he gave one of his large plantations to each of his grandsons; he left his granddaughters $10,000 each; and he left his daughter Mary Lee the use of Arlington House during her lifetime (thereafter the property would belong to the Lees' oldest son, Custis). All these provisions were fine; Custis practically ignored his son-in-law but certainly cared for the rest of the family and his slaves. Trouble was, the estate was not worth all that Custis gave away. As a consequence, Lee had to become a planter and try to manage the Custis properties well enough to generate the cash to give to his daughters.

43 White House on the Pamunkey River, a large plantation inherited by W.H.F. ("Rooney") Lee from his grandfather, G.W.P. Custis. This is how the house looked on May 17, 1862.

Brady Collection, Library of Congress

42 About slavery and race— Lee wrote candidly to his wife from Fort Brown (near Brownsville), Texas, on December 27, 1856. This is a copy of a portion of that letter. Having declared slavery "a moral & political evil in any country," Lee continued, "I think it however a greater evil to the white than to the black race, & while my feelings are strongly enlisted in behalf of the latter, my sympathies are more strong for the former. The blacks are immeasurably better off here than in Africa, morally, socially & physically. The painful discipline they are undergoing is necessary for their instruction as a race, & I hope will prepare & lead them to better things. How long their subjugation may be necessary is known & ordered by a wise, Merciful Providence. Their emancipation will sooner result from the mild & melting influence of Christianity, than the storms & tempests of fiery Controversy. This influence though slow is sure."

Letter is in the Virginia Historical Society

At that point, Lee discovered just how inefficiently Custis had operated his plantations. And then Lee discovered that Custis's slaves knew that they were supposed to be freed. The will stipulated that it should be within five years, but the African-Americans most involved did not know what the will said and believed they were being robbed.

Lee had owned slaves for most of his adult life; he inherited some from his mother, and in 1846, when he wrote his will, he still owned "Nancy & her children at the White House, New Kent." Now, however, Lee had to organize and supervise the Custis slaves living on three very large plantations so as to produce enough to sell for the cash to carry out the provisions of the will. Under the circumstances, it is not at all surprising that the Custis slaves resented their new "master." And Lee came to realize that he was not a very effective slaveholder. Throughout his life, he had shrunk from confrontation and conflict, and confrontation and conflict were inevitable in the slave-plantation system. "Nancy & her children" were hired out (rented); the slaves Lee now had in his charge were in effect his for the next five years. He did the best he could under the circumstances, but the best things he did were auditing the accounts of the managers of the various properties and installing honest, efficient people to run each operation.

All of this labor took time, and Lee had to extend his leave from the army until more than two years had passed. Of course Lee was concerned with Custis's will and managing the plantations, but the real question related to his future. He now had the opportunity to take charge of the Custis properties (perhaps 9,000 acres), make them profitable, and live in the style befitting his abilities and heritage. Lee called his quandary, "the question which I have staved off for twenty years."

On October 17, 1859, Lee was still at work on the Custis estate when a young lieutenant named J.E.B. Stuart interrupted him with a summons from the War Office. In this way, Lee became involved in the government's response to John Brown's raid on Harpers Ferry (in what would become West Virginia). Those who read about Brown and his blow against slavery rightly focus their attention upon Brown. Often overlooked in the story, however, is Lee's role in these events. He arrived at the scene, acquainted himself with the situation, secured the area around the fire-engine house, and planned his attempt to capture Brown. When he was ready, Lee launched his assault, which achieved his purpose in a very short time. Not only did Lee capture Brown; he did so with no harm to the thirteen hostages

44 | Romancoke in King William County, Virginia. This property belonging to George Washington Parke Custis, Lee's father-in-law, at Custis's death in 1857 passed to Robert E. Lee, Jr. ("Rob"). The 4,000-acre plantation earlier had been called Romancock. The name change occurred during the period of Lee's management as executor of the Custis estate and probably reflects Lee's sense of propriety.

Courtesy of Washington and Lee University

Brown was holding throughout the crisis.

Lee made his career decision sometime during the fall of 1859. He decided to remain in the army and to rejoin his cavalry regiment in Texas. In January 1860, Lee was back on the plains and apparently well satisfied to be there. He had turned his back upon the land and potential wealth in Virginia to continue his nomadic career in the army.

But of course Lee had no control over events that changed his prospects and his life. For a long while, he could only watch as the United States came apart. When Texas seceded from the Union, Lee left his post and returned to his family at Arlington House. Winfield Scott, then the commanding general of the United States Army, offered Lee command of the army being assembled to squelch the rebellion in the wake of the firing on Fort Sumter. Scott was too old and infirm to command in the field, and he wanted his protégé Lee to lead the troops in combat, if indeed it came to that. Shortly before Lee heard Scott's offer, the state of Virginia seceded from the Union (on April 17, 1861). Lee wrestled with himself intently but in the end turned down Scott.

Soon after Lee made his decision not to lead an army against his own people, the governor of Virginia offered Lee command of the armed forces of Virginia. Lee accepted.

These were momentous decisions that Lee made. He decided to turn his back on his oath to defend his country, and he decided to cast his lot with the slaveholders' republic, or at least with one member state of the slaveholders' republic. Many people have speculated about the reasons that drove Lee's decisions. Why did he act as he did? Had he accepted Scott's offer to command the field army that marched to put down the rebellion, Lee would have spent the rest of his life trying to explain his actions to those people about whom he cared the most—his relatives and friends in Virginia.

45 | Christ Church, Alexandria. Lee went here on Sunday morning, April 21, 1861, to meet Judge John Robertson and to receive from him a message from Virginia Governor John Letcher. The meeting miscarried, however, and Robertson sent Lee a note that evening requesting that he come to Richmond on April 22 to confer with Letcher. Photograph by E. T.

46 | The Right Reverend William Meade, who was rector of Christ Church, Alexandria, during the time when Robert Lee was growing up in that town and attending the church. Meade died in 1862 in Richmond. One story has the old bishop summoning Lee to his bedside, wishing him well in his war, and addressing him as "Robert." "I must call you Robert. I cannot call you 'General,'" Meade said, "I have heard your catechism too often." Courtesy of the Virginia Historical Society

He elected instead to cast his lot with those people about whom he cared most, even though he did not believe in the right of secession and did believe that slavery was a great evil. Lee cast his lot with the Confederacy out of respect for the feelings of his family and friends. In one sense, Lee chose to involve himself in the most horrendous war in American history because he did not like conflict. There is irony there somewhere. ❖

Arlington, Washington City P.O.
20 Apr 1861

Lt. Genl. Winfield Scott
Commd. U.S. Army

Genl

Since my interview with you on the 18th Inst: I have felt that I ought not longer to retain my Commission in the Army. I therefore tender my resignation which I request you will recommend for acceptance. It would have been presented at once but for the struggle it has cost me to separate myself from a Service to which I have devoted all the best years of my life, & all the ability I possessed. During that time, more than a quarter of a century, I have experienced nothing but kindness from my Superiors & the most Cordial friendship from my Comrades. To no one Genl have I been as much indebted as to yourself for uniform kindness & Consideration, & it has always been my ardent desire to meet your approbation. I shall carry with me to the grave the most grateful recollection of your kind Consideration, & your name & fame will always be dear to me. Save in the defence of my native State, I never desire again to draw my sword. Be pleased to accept my most earnest wishes for the Continuance of your happiness & prosperity, believe me

Most truly yours
R E Lee

47 A draft of Lee's resignation from the United States Army, April 20, 1861, addressed to Winfield Scott, Commander, with whom Lee had met two days earlier. Courtesy of the Museum of the Confederacy

48 Martha Custis Williams Carter, first cousin to Mary Lee and more distant cousin of Robert E. Lee, was Lee's confidante and correspondent for more than twenty-five years. Her brother was a sometimes-suitor of Agnes Lee. Here is a revealing passage from one of Lee's letters to "Markie," as she was called within the family.

> You have not written to me for nearly three months. And I believe it is equally as long since I have written to you. On paper Markie, I mean, on paper. But oh, what lengthy epistles have I indited to you in my mind! Had I any means to send them, you would see how constantly I think of you. I have followed you in your pleasures, & your duties, in the house & in the streets, & accompanied you in your walks to Arlington, & in your search after flowers. Did you not feel your cheeks pale when I was so near you? You may feel pale Markie; You may look pale; You may even talk pale; But I am happy to say you never write as if you were pale; & to my mind you always appear bright and rosy.

"Markie" only married in 1870, after Lee died. Courtesy of Tudor Place Foundation

49 George Washington Custis Lee ("Boo"), 1832–1913, oldest child and son in the Lee family. Custis finished first in his class at West Point, yet he seemed unable to get out from behind his father's shadow. Custis spent most of the war on the staff of President Jefferson Davis, even as he chafed to command troops. Courtesy of the Museum of the Confederacy

50 Mildred Childe Lee, youngest of the Lee children (born February 10, 1846; died 1905). Known as "Precious Life" within the family, Mildred was a delight to her father in his declining years.
Courtesy of the Museum of the Confederacy

51 Eleanor Agnes Lee ("Wigs"), fifth child (born February 27, 1841; died 1873) and third girl in the Lee family, Agnes became the "caregiver" in the household. Although she suffered from neuralgia herself, she was most often available to take care of her mother, and she accompanied her father on his "farewell tour" during the spring of 1870.
Courtesy of the Museum of the Confederacy

52 | William Henry Fitzhugh Lee, known as "Rooney," 1837–1891, the third child and second son of the Lees, was a mischievous lad. Rooney inspired Henry Adams to write his stereotypical characterization of Southerners whom Adams encountered at Harvard, where Adams and Rooney were classmates. "Strictly, the Southerner had no mind...." During the war, Rooney served as a cavalry officer under J.E.B. Stuart and rose to the rank of major general, the youngest in the Confederate Army. Courtesy of the Valentine Museum

53 | Mary Custis Lee, often called "Daughter," 1835–1918. Courtesy of Washington and Lee University

54 The United States Armory at Harpers Ferry. The fire-engine house in which John Brown held thirteen hostages and against which Lee launched the marines is on the left.

55 The restored fire-engine house on the arsenal grounds at Harpers Ferry. Here were John Brown, a few of his followers, and thirteen hostages on October 18, 1859. Lee directed the assault that captured Brown, killed some of his men, captured others, and did not harm any of the hostages.

Photograph by E. T.

56 | Main Street in Richmond in 1856. The city looked much like this when Lee came to command the Virginia armed forces in April of 1861. Courtesy of The Library of Virginia

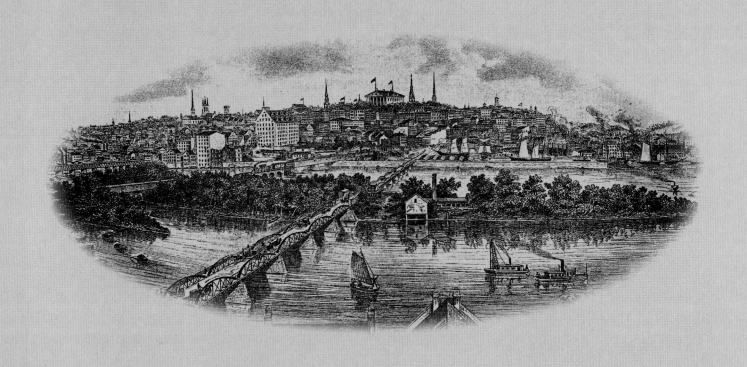

General Without an Army

4

Robert E. Lee's first task as commander of the armed forces of Virginia was to generate some armed force. It was Lee who had to organize the Virginia volunteers and militia units that in April and May of 1861 were flocking to the Southern banner. With a very small staff to help him, Lee succeeded in assembling, arming, organizing, and training about 40,000 soldiers. But as soon as these men were ready to serve, Lee had to surrender them to the Confederate Army for deployment. Because he performed his task so well, Lee was soon (summer 1861) without an armed force once again.

Because he commanded no troops, Lee saw no action in the initial clash of armies, the Battle of First Manassas (Bull Run). By this time (July 1861), however, Jefferson Davis had come to rely upon Lee for advice and counsel. And since Davis took seriously his constitutional role as commander-in-chief, Lee had the ear of a crucial person in strategic planning and wartime policy.

Late in July 1861, Davis dispatched Lee to a theater of the war that had become a significant problem for the Confederacy. Davis had lots of generals issuing orders in the Kanawha Valley (later part of West Virginia), but the situation there seemed bleak and not likely to improve. Lee went to the area to try to bring order and to improve command relationships among Generals John B. Floyd, Henry A. Wise,

58 | Mary Boykin Chesnut, author of a lively diary and wife of James Chesnut, who served as an aide to Jefferson Davis. On meeting Robert E. Lee, Chesnut recorded in her diary, "I like Smith Lee better, and I like his looks, too. I know Smith Lee well. Can anybody say they know his brother? I doubt it. He looks so cold and quiet and grand."

Courtesy of the Museum of the Confederacy

< **57** | A representation of Richmond before the war from the south side of the James River. Courtesy of the Library of Virginia

My coat is of gray, of the regulation style and pattern, and my pants of dark blue as is also prescribed, partly hid by my long boots. I have the same handsome hat which surmounts my gray head (the latter is not prescribed in the regulations) and shields my ugly face, which is masked by a white beard as stiff and wiry as the teeth of a [cotton] card. In fact, an uglier person you have never seen, and so unattractive is it to our enemies that they shoot at it whenever visible to them, but though age with its snow has whitened my head, and its frosts have stiffened my limbs, my heart you well know, is not frozen to you, and summer returns when I see you.

— Robert E. Lee's description of himself to his daughter-in-law, June, 1862

and William Wing Loring. Lee failed. Floyd and Wise, both former governors of Virginia and both effective statesmen, were not very competent warriors. But neither was aware of this flaw, so they feuded to the point at which Wise refused to follow Floyd's orders. Loring was a professional soldier and resented both Wise and Floyd. Loring outranked Lee in the "old" (United States) army, so he also resented Lee's advice in this campaign. Lee oversaw one aborted battle and acted as diplomatically as he was able, but he could not save the Kanawha Valley.

59 | A view of Lee's effects in a tent as he likely arranged and saw them during his campaigns. Courtesy of the Museum of the Confederacy, photograph by Katherine Wetzel

60 | Lee's personal effects. Courtesy of the Museum of the Confederacy, photograph by Katherine Wetzel

GENERAL WITHOUT AN ARMY

Lee returned to Richmond from the mountains on Halloween. He learned some negative lessons during the disjointed campaign and did two quite positive things: He grew his beard in the western Virginia mountains and wore it the rest of his life; he also found a horse that he particularly liked. When Lee first met him, the horse was four years old and named Jeff Davis. Lee expressed an interest in the animal then and encountered him again at his next place of duty in South Carolina. Now the horse was named Greenbrier. Lee purchased him for $200, renamed him Traveller, and rode him the rest of his life.

Lee did not remain in Richmond long; in less than a week, he was off to the South Carolina coast to command the Department of South Carolina, Georgia, and East Florida. Lee went south in response to a threat (the impending capture of Port Royal, South Carolina) and was able to do very little to counter that threat. He made the only wise choice under the circumstances: He withdrew the Confederate defenses up the rivers, exposing the barrier islands and coastal plain to the enemy and infuriating some of the most powerful people in the Confederacy. In March 1862, Lee returned to Richmond once more, having done his best under difficult circumstances.

Richmond was an uneasy capital during the spring of 1862. A Union army of 105,000 men, commanded by George B. McClellan, was assembling on the peninsula (between the James and York Rivers) and would eventually march on the capital. To defend Richmond against this peril, the Confederacy had General Joseph E. Johnston and an army about half the size of McClellan's.

Again Lee's assignment was to assist and advise President Davis. Joe Johnston was an old friend of Lee's; they had met at West Point and had been friends ever since.

61 | Wool felt hat belonging to Lee.
Courtesy of the Museum of the Confederacy, photograph by Katherine Wetzel

62 | Lee's spurs.
Courtesy of the Museum of the Confederacy

63 | Saddle blanket used on Traveller for a grand review of the Army of Northern Virginia.
Courtesy of the Museum of the Confederacy, photograph by Katherine Wetzel

64–65 These two photographs show the damage done to Fort Pulaski by the Federal bombardment in April 1862 with rifled artillery. In thirty hours, the fort that was supposed to be "as strong as the Rocky Mountains," pronounced "secure" by Lee, had fallen to the United States.

Brady Collection, Library of Congress

66 Fort Pulaski in recent times. The Confederate "Stars and Bars" is flying over the fort because filming of a "docudrama" was in progress. This is how Lee would have seen the fort when he inspected it in 1861 or 1862.

Photograph by E.T.

67 | Fort Pulaski, near the mouth of the Savannah River, the site of Lieutenant Lee's first work for the Army Corps of Engineers in 1829. Lee left here in 1831 to work at Fort Monroe in Virginia. He returned in early 1862 when the fort was completed and threatened by the United States. Lee assured the commander that Fort Pulaski was safe, but he did not factor in the rifled cannon, which compelled the Confederate garrison to surrender the fort after only thirty hours.

Courtesy of the National Park Service

But Johnston and Jefferson Davis were not friends and would never even come anywhere near friendship. Johnston became convinced that Davis was not supporting his efforts sufficiently and never would. Davis became convinced that Johnston was too timid and not exerting himself sufficiently. In this instance, Lee was squarely between these two jealous egos. On behalf of Davis he asked Johnston to come to see the president and to share his plans. On behalf of Johnston, Lee made excuses and offered only vague hints about what he intended to do to save Richmond and his army. The Confederacy was fortunate to have Lee available to buffer general from president, and vice versa.

Then, as the campaign before Richmond was approaching climax, Johnston suffered serious wounds at the Battle of Seven Pines (Fair Oaks) on May 31, 1862. Davis made about the only decision he could make, given the situation and the people involved: He appointed Lee commander of the Army of Northern Virginia.

The war was more than a year old, and Lee had never held a command in combat. Indeed, the only troops

Lee had ever commanded in combat were the marines who stormed the engine house at Harpers Ferry in October 1859. He had seen plenty of action, but always as a staff officer.

Lee learned a great deal during his year as a Confederate. He learned enough about the Confederate people and resources to know that they could not withstand a protracted war. He came to believe that the only chance the Confederacy had was to win the war in one campaign. Fight a battle of annihilation; destroy an enemy army. And do this sooner rather than later, because the longer the war lasts, the stronger the United States will become. Lee knew that Davis did not share this outlook; Davis believed that the Confederates could outlast their adversaries in a war of wills. Consequently, Lee as commander strove to achieve his battle of annihilation; all the while, he tried to keep Davis informed, but at a great enough distance from his headquarters so that Davis would not become involved in the strategy being plotted there. ❖

69 | The bar of the Spottswood House hotel in Richmond. Here habitués fought many a battle without losing a man; had the war gone the way these folks planned it, the Yankees would have quit within a few weeks. Lee reportedly told Georgia Senator Benjamin H. Hill that he had discovered a "fatal mistake" Southern statesmen had made when forming the Confederacy. Hill asked what the "fatal mistake" was, to which Lee responded, "Why, sir, in the beginning we appointed all our worst generals to command the armies, and all our best generals to edit newspapers." He spoke of the pains and energy he expended planning and fighting a battle. But sometimes defects appeared even in his most carefully laid plans. However, "[T]hese best editor-generals saw all the defects plainly from the start. Unfortunately, they did not communicate their knowledge to me until it was too late." Illustration from *Harper's Weekly*

68 | A letter from Beverly R. Codwise to Lee written in December 1861. Codwise says, "I enclose a letter from my mother telling me to come home, and not being able to stay in the army on account of my health I respectfully ask you to recommend me to Gen Jackson for a discharge as I would like to return home…" Such naiveté and such second thoughts about serving this new nation in a fight for its life doubtless made Lee wonder about the chances of success. Courtesy of the Virginia Historical Society

Annus Mirabilis

5

When Lee assumed command of the Army of Northern Virginia on June 1, 1862, the army and the would-be nation were in desperate straits. Betting persons would have given long odds against the Confederacy's surviving the summer. Then came Lee to command.

He reconstituted his army as best he could and planned to gain control of this campaign McClellan was waging. He gambled. Lee gambled desperately. And he won. He won the Seven Days' Battles and hurled McClellan's force from the suburbs of Richmond to Harrison's Landing under the cover of their gunboats, twenty-three miles from the capital. Lee then won Second Manassas (Bull Run) and sent the Federals once more streaming back to Washington in a panic. By the end of the summer, Lee had taken the offensive and marched into Maryland. At the same time, at Lee's prodding, another Confederate army marched into Kentucky. From the edge of extinction, the Confederacy had revived and was carrying the war to the enemy on two fronts.

Lee fought at Sharpsburg (Antietam) because he believed he could win. He was mistaken. The Confederacy nearly lost an army and possibly the war that September 17. But Lee made good his escape, and his army lived to fight another day. One of those days was December 13, 1862. On Marye's Heights, south of the town of Fredericksburg,

---

70 | This is how Chickahominy Swamp appeared in 1862 — and still does, for the most part. *From Battles and Leaders*

Alexander, if there is one man in either army, Federal or Confederate, who is, head and shoulders, far above every other one in either army in audacity that man is General Lee, and you will very soon have lived to see it. Lee is audacity personified. His name is audacity. . . .
— JOSEPH CHRISTMAS IVES to his comrade Edward Porter Alexander, June, 1862

Lee's army stood on the defensive and slaughtered the Federals now commanded by Ambrose E. Burnside. Fredericksburg restored Lee's dominance on the eastern front, and now many on both sides were convinced that one more campaigning season in 1863 would secure Southern independence.

Very early in the spring of 1863, Lee suffered what was probably the onset of angina, heart disease, and general cardiovascular troubles. No one diagnosed the problem, and Lee recovered somewhat from his "heavy cold" or lumbago or rheumatic chest pains.

At Chancellorsville, Lee won what many military historians consider his greatest victory. Once more Lee gambled; he placed his army in a position to lose it and the war on one afternoon. But Lee won; his gamble paid off. During all this time in which Lee had been winning battles and baffling his enemies, he was less delighted than many people then and now believe. Although he was winning, he was falling short of a great battle of annihilation. Each time the enemy escaped. Maybe the sort of battle that Lee envisioned was beyond possibility in the American Civil War.

Lee's most elaborate attempt to fight a battle big enough to win the war was at Gettysburg, in the afterglow of Chancellorsville. Stonewall Jackson had been a casualty at Chancellorsville—shot in the dark accidentally by some of his own troops, Jackson died a week later. Lee reorganized his army once again and marched north into Pennsylvania.

71 | White House, after George B. McClellan's army had evacuated the place and the general no longer needed the house for his headquarters. (*See* page 49)

The sunken road that became "Bloody Lane" at Sharpsburg (Antietam). Fighting and killing were furious here. *From Battles and Leaders*

He accepted battle at Gettysburg and endeavored to generate a "moment of truth" on the fields around that town. This time, Lee lost. Controversy continues over who did the most to influence the outcome of the battle one way or the other, but Lee himself proclaimed, "It's all my fault." Gettysburg may have been Lee's last chance to fight the huge battle he believed he had to fight.

Annus mirabilis means "year of wonders or miracles." Certainly this expression applies to Confederate arms after Lee came to command the Army of Northern Virginia. Here the "year" includes Gettysburg and thus becomes thirteen months of wonders. There is a reason for this. Including the Gettysburg campaign in the "year" allows the focus of Lee's strategy to remain where Lee left it—on the offensive in search of a victory complete enough to win the war. Lee persisted in his search for the climactic battle; he continued to try to destroy his enemies until he could try no more. However, Lee knew thereafter that winning would become more difficult. Gettysburg had been his last realistic opportunity to win the war as he believed he might. ❖

73 | James Ewell Brown Stuart —Lee's "eyes" during the war and his cadet during his service as superintendent of West Point.

Courtesy of the Museum of the Confederacy

74 | Joseph E. Johnston, Lee's friend from West Point days. Johnston evidenced envy during the war; he believed the Army of Northern Virginia was his army and resented Lee's retaining command after he (Johnston) recovered from the wounds he sustained at Seven Pines. "What luck some people have," Johnston wrote after Lee's victory at Fredericksburg. "No one would attack me in a place like that." Lee continued to like Johnston and believe in his capacity to command a significant Confederate army. Lee probably had the most to do with Johnston's getting command of the Army of Tennessee in December 1863. After Lee became the commander-in-chief of all Confederate armies, he soon called Johnston to resume command of the remnant force before Sherman in the Carolinas.

Brady Collection, Library of Congress

75 | Thomas Jonathan ("Stonewall") Jackson, Lee's most trusted lieutenant. Jackson shared Lee's insistence upon the offense and usually acted out aggressive strategy and tactics. Lee said of Jackson, "Such an executive officer the sun never shone on. I have but to show him my design, and I know that if it can be done it will be done. No need for me to send or watch him. Straight as the needle to the pole he advances to the execution of my purpose."

Courtesy of the National Archives

76 | The sunken road and stone wall near the base of Marye's Heights at Fredericksburg. Here Lee and the Army of Northern Virginia achieved an enormous victory over Ambrose E. Burnside's Army of the Potomac in 1862. Twelve times the Federals surged forward against the impregnable defensive position, and each time they faltered and fell in huge numbers. This was the battle that inspired Lee to muse, "It is well that war is so terrible. We should grow too fond of it."

Courtesy of the Library of Congress

77 | Cows and cannon on the battlefield at Sharpsburg (Antietam). Photograph by E. T.

78 | The Marye house on the heights south of Fredericksburg. This hillside was the anchor of Lee's line in the great battle of December 13, 1862.

Brady Collection, Library of Congress

79 | *Frank Leslie's Illustrated Newspaper*, October 4, 1862. The
Northern press acknowledges Lee. The text uses terms such as
"hauteur," mediocrity," and "vain ambition" to describe Lee.

80 | A sketch of Lee "in the
field"—the only one done
from life—by Frank Vizetelly. Courtesy of the
Virginia Historical Society

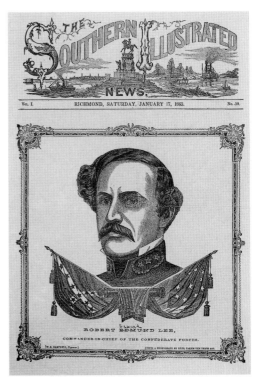

> **81** | Lee as most Confederates saw him. This print appeared in
The Southern Illustrated News, Richmond, January 17, 1863,
and was a variant of the photograph by Mathew Brady taken sometime
between 1850–52. Courtesy of the Museum of the Confederacy

82 An editorial cartoon from *Harper's Weekly*, August 30, 1862, depicting Lee's frustration at Federal General John Pope's aggressive policy toward civilians. Ironically, on the same day that the magazine appeared, Lee defeated Pope at Second Manassas (Bull Run).

83 Lee and Stonewall Jackson plotting the Battle of Chancellorsville.

From *Battles and Leaders*

84 | The foundation of the Chancellor House at the battlefield of Chancellorsville. To this spot on May 3, 1863, Lee rode in triumph. Charles Marshall of Lee's staff recalled the scene: "The scene is one that can never be effaced from the minds of those who witnessed it. The troops were pressing forward with all the ardour and enthusiasm of combat. The white smoke of musketry fringed the front of the line of battle, while the artillery on the hills in the rear of the infantry shook the earth with its thunder, and filled the air with the wild shrieks of the shells that plunged into the masses of the retreating foe. To add greater horror and sublimity to the scene, Chancellor House and the woods surrounding it were wrapped in flames. In the midst of this awful scene, General Lee... rode to the front of his advancing battalions. One long, unbroken cheer, in which the feeble cry of those who lay helpless on the earth blended with the strong voices of those who still fought, rose high above the roar of battle, and hailed the presence of the victorious chief. He sat in the full realization of all that soldiers dream of—triumph; and as I looked upon him in the complete fruition of the success... I thought that it must have been from such a scene that men in ancient days rose to the dignity of gods." Photograph by E.T.

85 | The Chancellor House as it appeared before the battle and before Lee rode in triumph into the yard. When Lee came here, the house was already ablaze. From *Battles and Leaders*

86 A 1987 photograph of what Lee saw from Seminary Ridge looking toward Cemetery Ridge on July 3, 1863, before Pickett's Charge.

Photograph by David Muench

87 Lee's headquarters at Gettysburg. When in the field, he often lived in the open air.

Brady Collection, Library of Congress

88 Cary Robinson. At an especially difficult time during the war, Lee received a note from "your two little friends" (young girls) requesting "our beloved Gen." to give Cary Robinson a furlough to spend Christmas with them. The two girls promised to pay Lee back in "thanks and love and kisses." As it happened, Lee knew Robinson and knew that he had recently lost his brother, and he took the time to write to Robinson to say he would have a furlough if possible and to extend his sympathy for the death of his brother. Then Lee wrote to his "two little friends" and told them what he had done. He added, "I fear I was influenced by the bribe held out to me, and will punish myself by not going to claim the 'thanks and love and kisses' promised me. You know the self denial this will cost me. I fear too I shall be obliged to submit your letter to Congress, that our Legislators may know the temptations to which poor soldiers are exposed, and in their wisdom devise some means of counteracting its influence. They may know that 'bribery and corruption' is stalking boldly over the land, but they may not be aware that the fairest and the sweetest are engaged in its practices." The torn label on the photograph says, "Killed in the War."

Courtesy of the Virginia Historical Society

89 Lucy Minnegerode, one of Lee's "two little friends" who wrote to their "beloved General" about spending Christmas with Cary Robinson. Her father was Charles Minnegerode, the rector of St. Paul's Church in Richmond.

Courtesy of the Virginia Historical Society

Stress and Socks

6

With the arrival of spring in 1864 came renewed fighting on a large scale, and to the Virginia theater of the war came Ulysses S. Grant. He had charge of all the Federal armies, but he chose to pitch his tent, so to speak, next to that of George G. Meade and personally direct operations against Lee. Grant remained in touch with his other armies via telegraph and letters.

During the winter of 1863–64, Lee fretted a great deal about the increasing disparity in men and materiel. And in fact, his army was usually outnumbered two-to-one in the battles that took place in 1864. Lee manifested his concern and his high degree of stress in one odd manner. He counted socks. Mary Lee, her daughters, and friends transformed the house on Franklin Street in Richmond into an "industrial school," as one visitor called the place, and knitted all manner of garments for the troops. Their specialty seemed to have been socks. When they had accumulated a significant number of pairs, Mary Lee sent them to her husband. She always indicated how many pairs of socks were in each of her bundles. And General Robert E. Lee, commanding general of the Army of Northern Virginia, responsible for the fate of the nation, the single general capable of winning battles on a regular basis, re-counted the pairs of socks sent to him by his wife. Sometimes he even counted them twice, and it was a good thing he did, because, as he once wrote to her, "The number of pairs scarcely ever agrees with your statement."

91 | Bones of those killed at Cold Harbor. This photograph was taken in April 1865. Brady Collection, Library of Congress

ON OPPOSITE PAGE

90 | Lee in full dress uniform with sash and sword; a J. Vannerson photograph made in early 1864.
Courtesy of the Valentine Museum

He found sixty-seven pairs instead of the sixty-four Mary wrote that she had sent. Something is dreadfully wrong with this picture. Generals have better uses for their time, or they certainly should have more important tasks to perform.

Lee counted socks. With the fate and weight of the nation upon his shoulders, Lee withdrew from the myriad problems about which he could do nothing, or at least nothing immediately effective, and did something he could control. He counted socks. Here was a pastime that had some conclusion and possessed a concrete, definitive solution. Here also is a pretty clear indication of the level of stress that beset Lee as the war wore on.

92 Looking into the "Mule Shoe" at Spotsylvania Court House. Photograph by E.T.

93 Here are the remains of a trench line from the Battle of the Wilderness with intrusions from more recent time. Photograph by E.T.

94 The site of the McCoull House at Spotsylvania Court House. Here Lee prepared to lead an infantry charge in the attempt to stem the Federal advance into the "Mule Shoe" salient. Cooler heads among Lee's staff and subordinates prevailed, called out, "Lee to the rear!" and turned Traveller around.

Photograph by E.T.

95 | Vicious fighting at the "Bloody Angle" in the "Mule Shoe" at Spotsylvania Court House. This was the sort of conflict that Lee proposed to join on those occasions when his men had to restrain him.

From *Battles and Leaders*

96 | A sketch of the McCoull House, where Lee was about to lead an infantry charge in an effort to keep the Federals from breaking through his lines in the "Mule Shoe." From *Battles and Leaders*

Grant came across the Rapidan River in May; Lee was ready for him. Here began the terrible series of battles that defined Grant's strategy during the spring of 1864. The two armies collided in the Wilderness and Lee won. At least he stopped his enemy and then attacked him in what one scholar has termed Lee's "last serious offensive stroke." Grant recoiled but did not retreat. Instead, he dispatched columns of soldiers south and east in an effort to get around Lee's army and cut it off from its base of supplies. Lee was too quick to allow Grant this advantage; he moved when Grant moved and anticipated Grant's destination. The result was Spotsylvania Court House, a heinous bloodbath that lasted for days. Then Grant moved again, and again he moved south and east. Lee met the invaders at the Annas—a series of rivers. Grant moved again, and this time he believed that he could drive a column through the center of Lee's long battle line. Lee was ready, and Grant lost at Cold Harbor (or Second Cold Harbor). By this time (June 3, 1864), Grant had lost at least 50,000 men—killed, wounded, or captured. Lee had lost far fewer, but the Confederacy could not afford even that loss.

Following his fiasco at Cold Harbor, Grant broke away. Lee did not know where his enemy had gone. As it happened, Grant did what Lee had feared other Union generals might do—cross the James River and move on Richmond from Petersburg, a rail junction about twenty-three miles south of the capital. Lee barely committed his troops in time to prevent the capture of Petersburg, and then both armies began to dig. From mid-June 1864, the war became a contest of trenches, and Lee was able to use his holes to save his army.

Eventually the trenches became too thinly held, and on April 2, 1865, Lee had to abandon Petersburg and Richmond and flee. His army only lasted for one week

> **97** | Lee on Traveller in a rare (perhaps unique) photograph of him "in the field." probably he was in Petersburg; the rubble indicates proximity to the war. Courtesy of Stratford Hall

STRESS AND SOCKS

in the open country. At last Lee's enemies were both in front of and behind him, and he had no option but to surrender. This he did at Appomattox Court House on April 9, 1865.

In the aftermath of Appomattox, Lee went to Richmond and there rallied his family. But soon he would have to decide what to do next. In the meantime, he took Mary and some of their daughters and spent the summer at Derwent, a small house west of Richmond that friends offered the defeated general. Amid many options came an election as president of Washington College. Lee thought about the offer and in the end accepted. He had sent many of the rising generation to their death or maiming. Now he would do something positive for these young men who had survived this terrible war. ❖

GRANT TURNING LEE'S FLANK.

98 | An editorial cartoon from *Harper's Weekly*, June 11, 1864. As it happened, Grant did turn Lee's flank, or get to the point that he could turn it; but it took him about nine months to do it.

> 99 | The surrender scene at Appomattox. Charles Marshall is the other Confederate. From *Battles and Leaders*

100 | Sketch by Alfred Waud of Lee and Charles Marshall riding away from the McLean House following the surrender, April 9, 1865.
Courtesy of the Library of Congress / Museum of the Confederacy

101 | A sketch of Lee at the McLean House at Appomattox by Thomas Nast. Courtesy of the Museum of the Confederacy

102 | The McLean House at Appomattox in April 1865.
Brady Collection, Library of Congress

103 | General Orders No. 9. Lee's farewell to

his army in the wake of Appomattox, written by Charles Marshall under Lee's guidance.

Courtesy of the Museum of the Confederacy

104 | The pen Lee used to surrender his army

at Appomattox in 1865.

Courtesy of the Museum of the Confederacy

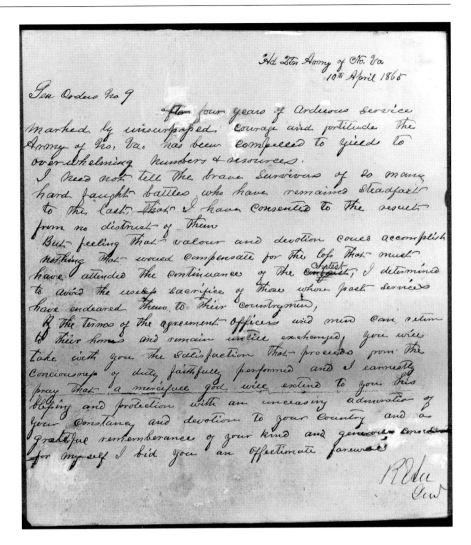

105 | The sword worn by Robert E. Lee at Appomattox.

Courtesy of the Museum of the Confederacy,

photograph by Katherine Wetzel

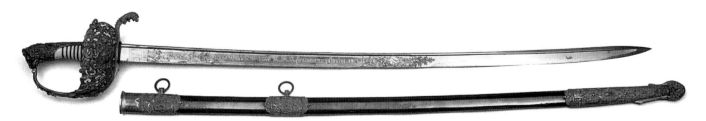

106 | G.W. Custis Lee,
Robert E. Lee, and Walter
H. Taylor at the house on Franklin Street
in Richmond on April 16, 1865.
Mathew Brady took this photograph.

Courtesy of the Virginia Historical Society

107 | The street where
Lee lived in Richmond.
The Lee house is second from
the left. Brady Collection, Library of Congress

108 Derwent, in Cumberland County, Virginia, due west of Richmond and about halfway between Richmond and Lynchburg. Here the Lees spent the summer of 1865. A friend "lent" this house to the family and furnished it sufficiently to render the place "habitable." Robert Lee seemed to enjoy the solitude, a relief from the stress and chaos of the previous four years. Other members of the family were not quite so content. Mary Lee, for example, called Derwent a "little retired place with a straight up house and the only beauty it possesses is a fine growth of oaks which surrounds it." As the hot summer wore on, she wrote of "a quiet so profound that I could even number the acorns falling from the splendid oaks that overshadowed the cottage."

Courtesy of the Museum of the Confederacy

Officer in Academe

7

Washington College was a tiny (fifty students in the fall of 1865), destitute school in Lexington, Virginia. The small town in the hills of the Shenandoah Valley, near the southern end, also was home to the Virginia Military Institute (VMI), which had sustained significant damage during the war. Washington College had escaped major destruction, but it needed help if the school were to survive. Surely this was one very good reason the trustees had elected Robert E. Lee as president and had gone to some lengths to try to persuade him to accept. The trustees were no doubt delighted when Lee appeared and took his oath as president. He also took an oath of amnesty to the United States in which he swore that he would support, protect, and defend the Constitution and the Union and would obey the laws passed during the rebellion, including those relating to the emancipation of slaves. Soon thereafter, the trustees learned that they had more president than they had expected.

Lee had been thinking about the best way to educate people for a long time—probably since his first experience in a classroom at West Point. He had some very good ideas that he wanted to put into practice, and few of those ideas had anything to do with the kind of education he had received and administered at the Academy.

The trustees undoubtedly believed that they had hired a nice old man who just happened to be a fourth member of the Trinity in the South, or perhaps a Moses not yet

110 | A postwar carte-de-visite.
Courtesy of Washington and Lee University

111 St. Paul's Episcopal Church, Richmond. Lee attended this church, which was literally and symbolically across the street from Capitol Square. Here Jefferson Davis received Lee's message that he would have to abandon Richmond within about twelve hours. And here, after the war, Lee joined an African-American at the communion rail and so brought grace to an otherwise awkward situation.

Courtesy of the Virginia Historical Society

112 The Reverend Charles Minnegerode, rector of St. Paul's Church, Richmond, from 1856 to 1889. Lee often attended St. Paul's Church when he was in Richmond. Jefferson Davis received Lee's fateful message that he would have to abandon Petersburg and Richmond while worshipping at St. Paul's on April 2, 1865. In June 1865 Lee attended St. Paul's and heard Minnegerode issue the invitation to the congregation to come to the chancel rail to receive communion. Then an African American man strode first to the front of the church. One witness described a pregnant pause that followed— Minnegerode seemed flustered and the would-be communicants were stunned and immobile. Lee quickly and quietly stood, strode forward, and knelt near the African American at the rail and so redeemed the moment. Courtesy of St. Paul's Church, Richmond

ready to enter the promised land, but a Moses nonetheless. He had said that he would not and could not teach. He would simply retire to the President's House and appear at the strategic moments to raise money and attract students. After all, his salary depended upon the number of students registered at the college. The trustees had courted and won the nineteenth-century equivalent of a "cash cow." All they needed to do was remind the old fellow when it was time for another recounting of the third Battle of Winchester, after which some of the youngsters would pass the hat for the college.

However, that was not the way Lee served the school. He was, within the limits of his health, a president involved with his institution. He attended chapel every day; he had advice for the crew at work on the new chapel; he made appointments to meet with students who had problems and counseled them; he persuaded the faculty to permit elective courses, to expand the curriculum to include more science courses, and to add more departments in "studies" such as law and journalism; and he had even more plans for a department of medicine, for example.

These things and more Lee did for his college. Yet to the surprise of many people, including Lee himself most likely, Lee did not generate much money for the school. He did persuade Cyrus McCormick to give some money, and he worked on some other wealthy men. But he did not endow Washington College on the strength of his name. Lee's major problem was time; he had so little of it left when he arrived at the school, and his stamina declined markedly during the final two years he was in Lexington.

The Lees had a pleasant life at the college. They lived in the President's House and then built another nearby and moved into it. They visited the various springs and spas during the summers. And Robert Lee certainly enjoyed his work while he was still able to do it.

> **114** Lee on Traveller in September 1866. Riding was then and throughout his life Lee's favorite form of exercise. He tried to ride every day that the weather permitted.

Courtesy of Washington and Lee University

113 Mary Custis Lee. She maintained a strong presence within the Lee family even as she suffered from crippling arthritis.

Courtesy of Washington and Lee University

All too soon, Lee's cardiovascular problems began to worsen, threatening his life. He became so weak that he could not walk from his office in the basement of the chapel to his home (admittedly up a hill) without stopping several times to rest. These buildings are not very far apart. In the fall of 1870, Lee suffered a stroke, lingered for about two weeks, and died.

Immediately the apotheosis commenced. ❖

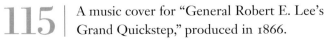

115 | A music cover for "General Robert E. Lee's Grand Quickstep," produced in 1866.

116 | The Colonnade at Washington
and Lee University—a recent view.

Photograph by E.T.

117 The Lee-Jackson House at Washington and Lee University. Once the President's House at Washington College, this house was the residence of Thomas Jonathan Jackson (later "Stonewall") after he married the daughter of the then-president of the college. Jackson was on the faculty of the Virginia Military Institute at the time. Lee lived here from 1865 until 1869, when he and his family moved into the new President's House nearby. Photograph by E.T.

118 The President's House, Washington and Lee University. This photo was taken soon after the house was constructed. Traveller's quarters are on the left. The porch was a modification in the original plans to accommodate Mary Lee's wheelchair.

Courtesy of Washington and Lee University

119 The President's House, as it now looks. Lee had a hand in designing this house, although the plan came from a "pattern book" popular at the time. Photograph by E.T.

120–121

The interior and the parlor (*right*) of the President's House at Washington College.

Courtesy of the Virginia Historical Society / Washington and Lee University

122 | Mary Tabb Bolling Lee, known as "Tabb," was Rooney's second wife. She was nineteen when she married Rooney, and she lived to the age of eighty-one. They married on November 28, 1867, in Petersburg, Virginia. Her father-in-law wrote to her mother-in-law that the wedding was quite a party and that the happy couple would likely not feel up to traveling as planned on the morning after the ceremony. Robert Lee attended—the first time he had been in Petersburg since the evening of April 2, 1865, when he left town rather hurriedly.

Courtesy of the Virginia Historical Society

123 | General Francis Smith, superintendent of the Virginia Military Institute (VMI), the "neighbor" to Washington College in Lexington, Virginia. Smith was not impressed with Lee's innovations in curricula and discipline; he referred to them as "twaddle." On occasions that required Lee to march with Smith in some ceremonial procession, Lee consistently walked out of step—so consistently that it could hardly have been coincidence. Lee may have been responding to Smith in this behavior, or he may have been responding to his distaste for military regimen. (He once said that the "great mistake" of his life was "taking a military education.") Most likely he was making a nonverbal statement about both Smith and the military. Courtesy of the Virginia Historical Society

124 | In August 1869, Lee joined a gathering of the rich and famous at White Sulphur Springs, West Virginia. Seated, left to right: Blacque Bey, Lee, George Peabody, W.W. Corcoran, and James Lyons. Standing, left to right: James Conner, Martin W. Gary, John B. Magruder, Robert D. Lilley, P.G.T. Beauregard, Alexander R. Lawton, Henry A. Wise, and Joseph L. Brent.

Courtesy of the Library of Virginia

125 Frank Buchser, a Swiss artist commissioned to paint the American Civil War, did this, the third of three Lee portraits "from life" during the Fall of 1869. Buchser submitted the painting as the fulfillment of his commission and protested that Lee was the most significant, most noble person to emerge from the war and thus the most important subject he could paint. The portrait languished in a Swiss warehouse for many years before a Swiss ambassador to the United States had it shipped to Washington and hung in the Swiss Embassy.

Courtesy of the Georgia Museum of Art

127 | Lee Chapel at Washington and Lee University. Lee was something of a "sidewalk superintendent" during the construction of the chapel. He was regularly present in the chapel at 8 a.m. every day, even after he made attendance voluntary for the students. Photograph by E. T.

128 | Lee's office in the basement of the Lee Chapel, preserved just as he left it on September 28, 1870. Photograph by E. T.

126 | Franz (later Frank) Buchser painted the last portrait of Lee from life in the Fall of 1869. Buchser was born in 1828 in Feldbrunnen, Switzerland. As a young man, he apprenticed with two piano-makers. The second caught his apprentice in bed with his daughter, and Buchser departed in haste for Paris. Soon thereafter, he traveled to Rome, served in the papal Swiss Guard, then joined the army of Giuseppe Garibaldi to fight for Italian independence. He returned to Paris to study art and continued to travel. Buchser traveled widely in America from 1866 to 1871. Lee was more candid and open with Buchser than with most people. Buchser said of Lee, "One cannot see and know this great soldier without loving him."

Courtesy of the Virginia Historical Society

Apotheosis

8

The image of Robert E. Lee—in the Southern mind, in the American mind, and in whatever cosmic world-class ranking system for hero-saints there is—is a fascinating study in itself. Thomas L. Connelly, in *The Marble Man: Robert E. Lee and His Image in American Society*, creates a catalog of varied images that he believes Lee has projected in the period since his death. Another scholar examining the materials Connelly consulted plus more (the corpus discovered and created in the two-plus decades since *The Marble Man* appeared) would probably conjure a whole new set of images and reveal even more than Connelly did about Lee and about the American mind.

Offered here is simply a sample. I have included some serious and I believe appropriate statues, paintings, and other traditional icons. I have also included some wonderful items that qualify as kitsch.

130 Recumbent statue of Lee in the Lee Chapel at Washington and Lee University. Edward V. Valentine originally intended to do a bust of Lee and made sketches and took measurements in May of 1870.

Courtesy of Washington and Lee University

ON OPPOSITE PAGE

129 Statue of Lee by Edward V. Valentine placed in the United States Capitol in 1934.

Courtesy of the Library of Virginia

Some materials defy fair representation in only two surfaces; it is all but impossible to display them on the pages of a book. One of these wonders is the Pickett's Charge Ball Point Pen. Within the barrel of the pen is a kinetic scene—Confederate soldiers "charge" if the pen is elevated at one end, and they fall back if the pen is elevated at the other end. In the scene also is a general on a white horse—Lee, of course.

My other favorite is one of those globes filled with water and a display—in this case, a Pickett's Charge diorama with a Lee figure watching the action. The reason I like this treasure so much, though, is the "snow" that falls whenever someone shakes the globe. I can only marvel at snow falling on Gettysburg, Pennsylvania, on July 3, 1863.

My own contribution to this genre—low culture in celebration of Lee—is a collection of limericks I have composed over time about Lee and his life. Here they are.

This first one refers to the shame that Light-Horse Harry bequeathed his son and that I believe conditioned much of Robert Lee's life:

> There once was a young man named Lee
> A frustrated sibling was he
> Son of an old hero
> With cash-flow sub-zero
> And a blight on the family tree.

This limerick is about Lee's relationship with his wife—definitely from Lee's perspective:

> There once was a young man named Lee
> A frustrated husband was he
> Was conjugal justice
> Life with Mary Custis?
> Let no one say dowries are free.

131 A drawing by Thomas Nast playing upon the reunion theme—Lee's image combined with Lincoln's words. Courtesy of Stratford Hall

> **132** "The Last Meeting" between Lee and Stonewall Jackson before Jackson's mortal wounds at Chancellorsville. Everett B.D. Julio did this in 1864; it became an icon of the "Lost Cause." Courtesy of the Museum of the Confederacy, photograph by Katherine Wetzel

This is about the boredom of Lee's tasks as an engineer during the early years of his career:

There once was a young man named Lee
A frustrated soldier was he
Never the bold dragoon
An engineer jejune
Condemned to drop rocks in the sea.

Lee was blessed in his ability to make the best of any circumstance in which he found himself. He also once confessed, "I am always wanting something." This poem is my attempt to reconcile Lee's wants with his capacity to find the best resolution for any situation:

133 Mary Custis Lee tinted this photograph very soon after her husband died.

Courtesy of Washington and Lee University

134 | From left: Miss Minnie Lloyd, Mary Custis Lee, Mrs. Sidney Smith Lee, and Mrs. William Henry Fitzhugh.

Courtesy of Washington and Lee University

135 | "Pres." G.W.C. Lee, made president of what soon after his father's death became Washington and Lee University. Custis Lee neither wanted nor liked his role as leader of the school. He tried to resign —unsuccessfully—on several occasions. What Custis likely wanted to do was teach chemistry at Virginia Military Institute (VMI). Courtesy of Washington and Lee University

136 | Mary Custis Lee, often called "Daughter," was the rebel in the family, but at least she was intensely proud in later life that she became the last surviving child of General Lee. Courtesy of the Museum of the Confederacy

137 | Mary Custis Lee as an old woman. She continued to live in the President's House at the college after her husband died, but she survived him by only three years. Courtesy of Washington and Lee University

Robert Lee sought something indeed.
"I'm always wanting something," he decreed.
But he tried really hard
Like the Rolling Stones bard
And found that you get what you need.

Many portray Lee as obsessed with control and discipline. Yet abundant evidence indicates that Lee was much more "modern" in the theology he practiced (as opposed to what he preached). One of those "somethings" Lee was always wanting was freedom, and he responded to individuals in ways far more loving than the moral platitudes he often recited:

Though evangelically idyllic,
Pious, and Virginiaphilic,
Not God, he was Lee
No Puritan he,
The Paul he resembled was Tillich.

Lee continues to appear in American life and popular culture. He stands for all manner of things—sometimes for the American South, often for those virtues associated with the South, or the past, or individuals commonly accepted as noble or virtuous. Such is the function of Lee-figures in life. Such is one of the uses of history. ❖

138–139 Statue of Lee by Jean Antoine Mercie on Monument Avenue in Richmond, Virginia, unveiled on May 29, 1890, amid appropriate fanfare. The base bears only the word "Lee," on the assumption that everyone would know who "Lee" was. Photograph by E. T.

140 Montgomery C. Meigs, quartermaster-general of the Union Army and from the Lee perspective the despoiler of Arlington House. Meigs assisted Lee in his engineering assignments on the Mississippi River during the 1830s; the two men went to St. Louis together to launch the projects in 1837, and Meigs drew many of the maps in accord with Lee's survey data. As quartermaster-general, Meigs was in charge of cemeteries for the graves of Federal soldiers who died in the service of their country. He used the Arlington estate, seized by the government for taxes unpaid. By the close of the war, Meigs had filled the grounds around the house with graves and thus rendered the place all but uninhabitable. Lee registered a complaint but trod lightly on the matter in the midst of ill will that afflicted many people in the aftermath of the war. Eventually Custis Lee managed to secure $150,000 from the government as compensation for the property.

Brady Collection, Library of Congress

141 The Lee family crypt in the basement of the Lee Chapel at Washington and Lee University. After this photograph was taken, Annie's remains were moved to the crypt from Warrenton, North Carolina. Courtesy of Washington and Lee University

142 | Tomb of Phillip Sheridan in the front yard of Arlington House. This was a significant indignity; Sheridan was an especially zealous foe and the enemy of cows, pigs, chickens, horses, corn cribs, barns, and anything else that provided aid and comfort to civilian Virginians. Courtesy of the Virginia Historical Society

143 | An early view of Arlington National Cemetery— sketched for Harper's Weekly in the Spring of 1869 by Theodore R. Davis.

Courtesy of the Virginia Historical Society

144 | Painting of Lee by Theodore Pine in 1904. This work is likely the best portrait of Lee done in the twentieth century.

Courtesy of Washington and Lee University

145 | Hofbauer mural of Lee and subordinates. Painted for "Battle Abby," now the Virginia Historical Society headquarters.

Courtesy of the Virginia Historical Society

146 Douglas Southall Freeman, editor of the *Richmond News-Leader*, radio commentator, and Pulitzer Prize-winning (1935) biographer of Robert E. Lee. Freeman wrote four volumes of *R.E. Lee: A Biography* and later three volumes of a history of the command of the Army of Northern Virginia, *Lee's Lieutenants: A Study in Command*. Still later Freeman wrote a seven-volume biography of George Washington—all while he edited a major daily newspaper, delivered fifteen minutes of comments on the news by radio each day (note the radio microphone at the left in front of the window), and gave numerous lectures throughout the United States. When Freeman completed his biography of Lee, his wife noticed that he seemed out of sorts and depressed for several days. She was reticent to "inquire after a gentleman's health," but finally she had to know what was wrong with her husband, and so she asked. Freeman apologized for his morose mood and explained that after spending twenty years in the company of Lee, it was only natural for him to be sad to leave so noble a soul.

Courtesy of the Virginia Historical Society

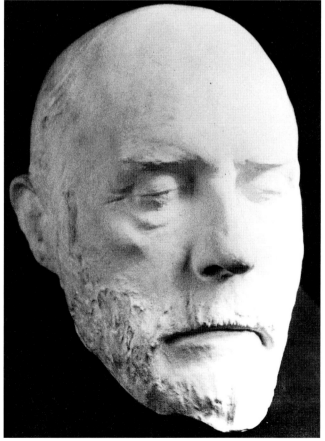

147 The death mask of Robert E. Lee.

Courtesy of the Museum of the Confederacy

148 | "Lee Feeds" for poultry and livestock, 20 percent laying mash.

Courtesy of Michael Parrish

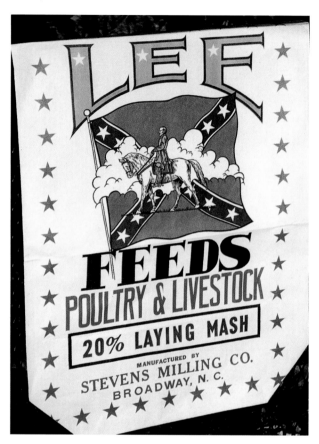

149 | Faux five-dollar bill with Lee's picture where Abraham Lincoln's should be and Stratford Hall on the reverse side.

150 | In keeping with the cigar fad of the late 1990s, here is a Robert E. Lee cigar. Ironically, Lee never smoked and advised his sons to abstain. Photograph by E.T.

151 | A figurine confused. The white beard makes this little ceramic fellow appear to be Lee. But the coat is blue, instead of gray, and the man is holding a cigar. We have here a peculiar amalgam of Lee and Ulysses S. Grant. Photograph by E.T.

Mary Lee becomes "Mary Anne Lee," and Mildred Childe Lee becomes "Childe."
Somehow a representation of Lee in his underwear seems inappropriate.

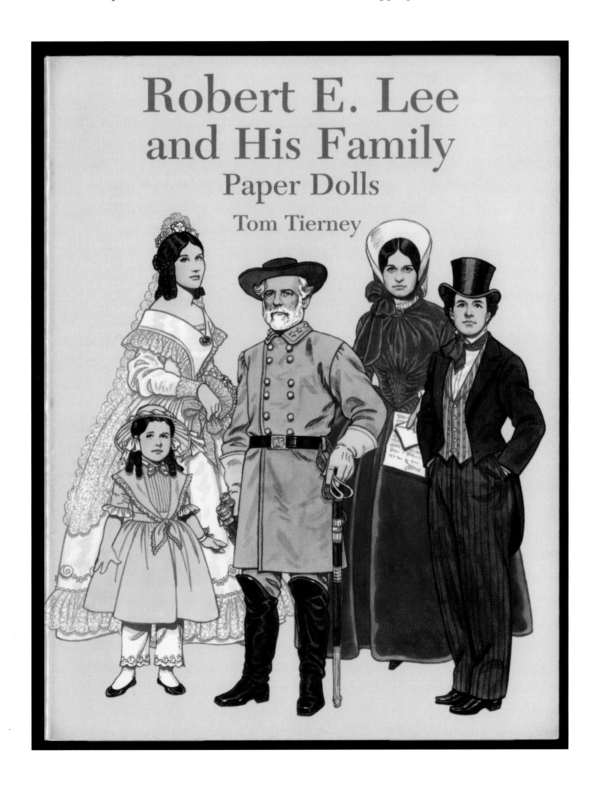

Robert E. Lee
and His Family
Paper Dolls
Tom Tierney

153 | Recumbent statue of Lee in snow by students of Washington and Lee University.

Courtesy of Washington and Lee University

154 | Grave of Traveller, just outside the Lee Chapel at Washington and Lee University in Lexington, Virginia. Various offerings (apples, carrots, et al.) have been left for Lee's war horse by students, tourists, and others. Photograph by E. T.

What could he want that he had never had?

He only said it once—the marble closed—
There was a man enclosed within that image.
There was a force that tried Proportion's rule
And died without a legend or a cue
To bring it back. The shadow-Lees still live.
But the first-person and the singular Lee?

The ant finds kingdoms in a foot of ground
But earth's too small for something in our earth,
We'll make a new earth from the summer's cloud,
From the pure summer's cloud.

                        It was not that,
It was not God or love or mortal fame.
It was not anything he left undone.
—What does Proportion want that it can lack?
—What does the ultimate hunger of the flesh
Want from the sky more than a sky of air?

He wanted something. That must be enough.

Now he rides Traveller back into the mist.

— STEPHEN VINCENT BENET, *John Brown's Body*

Robert Edward Lee—
A Chronology

1807–1870

Early Years

❖ Born January 19, 1807, at Stratford Hall, Virginia, to Ann Carter Lee and Henry ("Light-Horse Harry") Lee, the fourth child, third son, of Light-Horse Harry's second marriage. Robert had two half-siblings; his father's first wife had died.

❖ On April 24, 1809, Light-Horse Harry Lee went to jail for debt.

❖ During the summer of 1810, the Lees moved to Alexandria, Virginia, into a house owned by a generous member of the family.

❖ On the night of July 28, 1812, Light-Horse Harry Lee suffered grievous injuries at the hands of a mob in Baltimore while defending a friend's right to publish views opposed to the War of 1812 and the administration of President James Madison.

❖ In the summer of 1813, Robert's father sailed away to the West Indies, never to return to his home or family. He died en route home at Dungeness, the home of his Revolutionary War comrade Nathanael Greene on Cumberland Island, Georgia, on July 25, 1818. He was sixty-two years old.

Academy and Early Military Service

- In July 1825, Robert Lee enrolled in the United States Military Academy at West Point, New York.

- In June 1829, Lee graduated from West Point, ranked second in his class, and accepted a commission in the Corps of Engineers.

- On July 26, 1829, Lee's mother died at the age of fifty-six.

- In November 1829, Lee arrived at Cockspur Island near Savannah, Georgia. He was engaged in preparing the foundation of what became Fort Pulaski, which commanded the mouth of the Savannah River.

- In spring 1831, Lee moved to a new assignment at Fort Monroe, Virginia.

- On June 30, 1831, Lee married Mary Custis, only child of Mary and George Washington Parke Custis, at Arlington House, the Custis home built on land inherited from Custis's grandmother, Martha Washington, wife of the first president.

- Between 1832 and 1846, Mary and Robert Lee had seven children, all of whom survived into adulthood.

- In November 1834, Lee began an assignment as assistant to the Chief of the Engineer Corps. Since Lee now worked in the War Department in Washington, D.C., he and his family moved to Arlington House and lived with Lee's in-laws.

- In 1836 Lee earned promotion to first lieutenant.

- From 1837 to 1840, Lee spent considerable time in St. Louis moving the channel of the Mississippi River and creating a passage through the Des Moines and Rock River Rapids to extend navigation of the river farther upstream.

- In 1838, Lee earned promotion to captain.

- Lee served on the staff of General Winfield Scott in the Mexican War. He contributed significantly to Scott's campaign from Veracruz to Mexico City and earned the general's praise as the "very best soldier I ever saw in the field."

- Lee received three brevet (temporary) promotions for his service in Mexico and returned to the United States a colonel.

- From 1852 to 1855, Lee was superintendent of West Point.

- On July 17, 1853, Lee was confirmed in the Episcopal Church (with two of his daughters) at Christ Church, Alexandria, Virginia.

- In 1855, Lee transferred his branch of service in the army from engineers to cavalry and left West Point for the Texas plains and second-in-command of a regiment of horse soldiers.

- In October 1857, G.W.P. Custis, Lee's father-in-law, died at Arlington House. Lee was executor of a very confused estate and took extended leave from the U.S. Army in order to pursue his duties.

155 | photograph of Lee taken in 1850–52, age 43–45, before he became superintendent of West Point. Photograph by Mathew Brady.

War Years

- On October 17, 1859, Lee was still working on the affairs of the estate when he assumed command of two companies of marines and traveled to Harpers Ferry to quell a disturbance created by a person later identified as John Brown.

- On October 18, 1859, Lee commanded an assault upon a fire-engine house and captured John Brown without any harm to Brown's thirteen hostages.

- In January 1860, Lee returned to Texas and watched the election of Abraham Lincoln and the secession crisis unfold.

- On April 17, 1861, the state of Virginia seceded from the United States. The next day, Lee refused the opportunity to command the United States army that would act to put down the rebellion of Southern states—the self-proclaimed Confederate States of America.

- On April 22, 1861, Lee accepted command of "the military and naval forces of Virginia," and so joined the rebellion.

- On August 31, 1861, the Confederacy made Lee a full general, one of eight, in the Confederate Army.

- From July 28 until late October 1861, Lee served as a quasi-consultant to those in command of Confederate forces in western Virginia (now West Virginia). He witnessed the loss of the valley of the Kanawha River and great chaos among Southern "political" generals.

- On November 6, 1861, Lee became commander of the military Department of South Carolina, Georgia, and East Florida and set out for his command.

- From November 1861 to March 1862, Lee presided over more gloom for the Confederates and alienated many substantial citizens by moving defensive positions inland and acknowledging that he lacked the resources to defend the Southern coast.

- In March 1862, Lee became an adviser/chief of staff for Confederate President Jefferson Davis and mediated a stormy relationship between Davis and General Joseph E. Johnston, who commanded the army attempting to defend Richmond.

- On June 1, 1862, Lee became commander of the Army of Northern Virginia after Johnston suffered wounds the previous day. Here began the "annus mirabilis" for Lee and the Confederacy.

- In the Seven Days' Battles—June 25 to July 1, 1862—Lee drove Union General George B. McClellan from the suburbs of Richmond to a sanctuary twenty-three miles away.

- At Second Manassas (Bull Run) on August 30, 1862, Lee swept the Federal Army of the Potomac from the field and almost destroyed it.

- Then Lee invaded Maryland and counseled Davis to send the Confederacy's western army into Kentucky. From the brink of defeat, the Confederacy had armies on the offensive on two fronts.

- Sharpsburg (Antietam) on September 17, 1862, was the single bloodiest day of the entire Civil War and the end of Lee's offensive; he was fortunate to escape with his army intact.

156 A carte-de-visite or calling card known as the "floppy tie" pose among those who specialize in images of Lee. Lee's bow tie looks about to come untied.

Courtesy of the Library of Virginia

- At Fredericksburg on December 13, 1862, Lee stood on the defensive and inflicted terrible casualties upon his foes. At the close of the campaigning season, Lee's army was very much alive and dangerous, and his enemies seemed no closer to quashing the rebellion than they had been a year earlier.

- At Chancellorsville on May 1, 2, and 3, 1863, Lee achieved what may have been his greatest victory, but he lost his most valuable lieutenant, Thomas J. "Stonewall" Jackson.

- Lee led the Army of Northern Virginia north once more in June 1863 and collided with the Federals at the small town of Gettysburg. In furious fighting on July 1, 2, and 3, 1863, Lee failed to drive out or destroy his enemies. He limped home a loser.

- Campaigns in the fall of 1863 at Bristow Station and Mine Run displayed Lee and his army still capable of delivering significant blows.

- With the campaigns of 1864 came Ulysses S. Grant and renewed challenges.

- At the Wilderness (May 5–7, 1864), Spotsylvania Court House (May 7–19), North Anna (May 23–26), and Second Cold Harbor (June 1–3), Lee's army repulsed the Federals but had to give ground nonetheless.

- After Second Cold Harbor, Grant's forces seemed to disappear. They "reappeared" at Petersburg, a crucial railroad hub twenty-three miles below Richmond.

- Lee responded and held Petersburg. Then he began another phase of brilliance with his use of trenches to keep a superior force at bay. The two armies remained essentially in place from mid-June 1864 to April 2, 1865.

- On April 2, 1865, Lee realized that he had to abandon his trenches and flee in an attempt to save his army.

- At Appomattox Court House, on April 9, 1865, Lee surrendered to Grant. In public at least, Lee committed himself to restoring the Union and healing the wounds of the war.

Post-War Years

- After casting about for a role for himself in the defeated South, Lee accepted the presidency of Washington College in Lexington, Virginia.

- Lee became a very good educator and transformed a struggling college into a "modern" university. The school became Washington and Lee University soon after Lee's death.

- Lee suffered from cardiovascular troubles during the latter stages of the war (from April 1863), and his misdiagnosed illness plagued him as he sought to do the work of his college.

- On September 28, 1870, after returning home from a three-hour vestry meeting over which he presided, Lee suffered what was most likely a stroke.

- Lee lingered in a torpor for about two weeks and died on October 12, 1870.

- Apotheosis commenced almost immediately, and Lee continues to be an icon in American, and especially Southern, culture.

Index

PAGE NUMBERS IN *bold italics* REFER TO CAPTIONS.

For SAMUEL TALIAFERRO THOMAS *and* JULIA MARLENE THOMAS